Linda Sutton, MA

Love Matters
A Book of Lesbian Romance and Relationships

"Linda Sutton's newspaper column *Love Matters* was an important political statement during the turmoil of Colorado's Proposition 2, the anti-gay amendment. And now her book, a collection of these columns, gives readers outside of Colorado an opportunity to enjoy Sutton's wit, good sense, and tenderness about things relational. She may call herself a 'relationship fanatic' but that only means she cares about those things that are crucial to the survival and stability of lesbian relationships. Whether she is writing about dating, the death of a partner, or learning how to play and fight, Sutton is intelligent, compassionate, and nonjudgmental. And she's funny. That's a hard combination to beat."

Judith McDaniel
Author of *The Lesbian Couples Guide*

"There is for many a certain gift that makes relationships different—boundaries dissolve then reassert themselves after another is already within—the heart becomes confused and calls for exactly that blessing which Linda Sutton offers when only love makes any sense at all."

Stephen and Ondrea Levine
Authors of *Who Dies?* and *Embracing the Beloved*

Harrington Park Press
An Imprint of The Haworth Press, Inc.

Love Matters
A Book of Lesbian Romance and Relationships

HAWORTH Innovations in Feminist Studies
Esther Rothblum, PhD and Ellen Cole, PhD
Senior Co-Editors

New, Recent, and Forthcoming Titles:

Love Matters
A Book of Lesbian Romance and Relationships

Linda Sutton, MA

Harrington Park Press
An Imprint of The Haworth Press, Inc.
New York • London

Published by

Harrington Park Press, an imprint of The Haworth Press, Inc., 10 Alice Street, Binghamton, NY
13904-1580

"Dumpling Girl" by Dorothy Allison from *The Women Who Hate Me: Poetry 1980-1990*. Copy-
right © 1991 by Dorothy Allison. Reprinted by permission of Firebrand Books, Ithaca, New
York; "To Beth On Her Forty-Second Birthday" first appeared in *Warrior at Rest*, by Jane Cham-
bers (TNT Classics, Inc.). Copyright © 1984 by Jane Chambers. Reprinted by permission of Beth
Allen, 402 Fifth Street, Greenport, New York 11944; "If you lose your lover" by Judy Grahn.
Reprinted from *The Work of a Common Woman* (St. Martin's Press). Copyright © 1978 by Judy
Grahn. Reprinted by permission of the author; "July Morning" by Patti Grimes. Previously un-
published. Printed by permission of the author; "Love Is Not One of Those Countries Where You
Can Be Sure of the Weather" and "Living Together" by Jacqueline Lapidus. Copyright © 1975,
1997 by Jacqueline Lapidus. Reprinted by permission of the author; "Woman" from *The Black
Unicorn* by Audre Lorde. Copyright © 1978 by Audre Lorde. Reprinted by permission of W. W.
Norton & Company, Inc.; "Will I Still Wonder" from *Body of Love* by Judith McDaniel. Copy-
right © 1995 by Judith McDaniel. Reprinted by permission of the author; "The Heart Balloon"
from *Upstairs in the Garden: Poems Selected and New—1968-1988* by Robin Morgan. Copyright
© 1990 by Robin Morgan. Reprinted by permission of Edite Kroll Literary Agency; "Staying
Together" by Minnie Bruce Pratt from *We Say We Love Each Other*. Copyright © 1985 by Minnie
Bruce Pratt. Reprinted by permission of Firebrand Books, Ithaca, New York; "Fragment of a
Night" by Naomi Replansky from *The Dangerous World* (Another Chicago Press). Copyright ©
1994 by Naomi Replansky. Reprinted by permission of the author; "Jealousy" by Pamela Sneed.
Copyright © 1995 by Pamela Sneed. Reprinted by permission of the author.

The artwork in this book and on its cover was created by Jenny Faw and Jenny Faw Designs,
29 W. 19th Street, 4th Floor, New York, New York 10011.

Cover design by Marylouise E. Doyle.

The Library of Congress has cataloged the hardcover edition of this book as:

Sutton, Linda.
  Love matters : a book of lesbian romance and relationships / Linda Sutton.
    p.   cm.
  Includes bibliographical references.
  ISBN 0-7890-0288-4 (alk. paper)
    1. Lesbianism—United States. 2. Advice columns—United States. I. Title.
HQ75.6.U5S87 1999
306.76′63′0973—dc21   98-41558
                                                                              CIP

ISBN 1-56023-918-2 (pbk.)

FOR MAUREEN
without whom there would be no book
truly, madly, deeply

Oh, I could drink a case of you, darling
And I would still be on my feet.

Joni Mitchell
"A Case of You"
Blue

ABOUT THE AUTHOR

Linda Sutton, MA, is a feminist psychotherapist in private practice, educator, and consultant in Colorado Springs, Colorado. Throughout her career, she has lectured, written, lobbied, and advocated for issues of concern to women, children, and families. Ms. Sutton is the author and founder of the "Love Matters" column in the Colorado Springs lesbian newspaper *New Phazes,* and, with her partner, conducts "Love Matters" workshops on lesbian relationships.

CONTENTS

Acknowledgments

My life is abundant, meaningful, and infinitely blessed, even on days when I feel completely ungrateful. I have a loving family, many close and deep friendships, challenging and immensely rewarding work, reasonably good health (menopause aside), dogged persistence, a rich and complex (albeit neurotic) internal world, the best girlfriend in the universe, and a beautiful home in the breathtaking landscape that is Colorado. All of these elements of my life have combined in a synergistic and quite magical way to produce *Love Matters*. I give thanks for all of this.

I am particularly grateful to:

- my beloved life partner, Maureen Stevens, who collaborated with me on *every* aspect of writing this book—from being in a day-to-day relationship with me, to critiquing *each* version of *every* column, to holding me when I cried in frustration over the book, to rejoicing with me at its successes. Maureen is my biggest fan, my most steadfast supporter, and my inspiration as concerns *love matters*.
- my beautiful and precious daughter, Misty Eichengreen, who loves and accepts all of who I am—even when that makes her life more difficult.
- my mother, Betty Davison, sister Phyllis Bond, and brother and sister-in-law David and Sandi Kleinman, who are loving, proud, and loyal despite the radical and alternative ways I have chosen to think and live.
- my darling friend and savior Anita Anthony-Huebert (aka Tushy Baby) who edited this book—adding punctuation, correcting grammar, infusing politics and humor; who became a permissions editor searching for copyright holders; who crafted the most creative letters begging complete strangers for favors; who, on one of my bleakest days, counseled me to make chicken soup instead of killing myself. Her assistance was a Goddess-send.

- three other dear, faithful friends, Bonnie Poucel, Claudia Matthews, and Mark Clinton, who were there on a *daily* basis, following the progress of this book, holding my hand, discussing relationship theory with me *on demand*, cheering me on whenever I got stuck, believing in me to the end.
- an inner circle of other close and supportive friends whose continuous interest and encouragement was comforting and sustaining.
- a host of women who, in the great feminist tradition, went out of their way to provide help and assistance wherever and whenever it was needed to help ensure the success of this book: Suzanne Keating, Robin Morgan, Karen Huff, Julia Fitz-Randolph, Marcia Westkott, Katherine Pease, Jackie St. Joan, Nina Sokol, Jane Ragle, Clare Coss, D. J. Ross, Judith McDaniel, Lucinda Green, and Mary Reeves among many, many others.
- my clients who submitted many questions to the column, gave me terrific feedback, and encouraged and inspired me again and again.
- Jenny Faw for the fabulous artwork (which appears throughout this book and on its cover) as well as her incredible assistance with the *Love Matters* greeting card line.
- the staff, as well as the readership, of *New Phazes,* who made the column possible.
- The Haworth Press for giving a novice with some unconventional ideas and an unusual format her first opportunity to publish a book.
- and last, but not least, to the Goddess herself for making my very life possible.

But when we look on our lives and the world with a little keener awareness and deeper compassion, we see that amidst the suffering and confusion, the conflicts and attempts at escape, even a millisecond of love is a miracle.

Stephen Levine
Healing into Life and Death

The Beginning

Hello. My name is Linda, and I'm a relationship fanatic. I eat, drink, and sleep relationships—on the job, in the home, in much of my spare time. In fact, *lesbian love*—thinking about it, talking about it, living it (as I do daily with my beloved partner, Maureen)—is perhaps my greatest passion in life. So now I even get to *write* about it, in a monthly question-and-answer column, lesbian *Love Matters*. Sort of like having your cake and eating it too.

My perspective may be slightly different from some of my lesbian sisters (whose lesbianism was determined at birth) because, as a radical feminist from the 1970s, I chose lesbianism after a young adulthood spent living the alternative. Yes, I've *chosen* lesbianism (over and over again, I might add). We former heterosexuals may be a well-kept secret in some circles (and some might prefer we stay that way), but I'm having *way* too much fun in my thirteen-year relationship with Maureen not to share this secret with others. In lesbianism I have found my spiritual, emotional, and sexual center, and that compels me to write about the truth of my lesbian experience.

Women are relational by nature—highly concerned, if not consumed, with those they love. It's therefore no surprise that relationship questions are a hot topic of conversation among all lesbians I know. "Why are so many lesbian relationships so short-lived?" "What always happens to the *sex* in lesbian *sex*uality?" "What impact does homophobia have on intimacy?" "Can you sleep with a man and still call yourself a lesbian?" "What makes relationships so damn hard, anyway?" These are the kinds of issues being raised day in and day out in my psychotherapy practice, in bed at night with Maureen, on the phone for hours with my girlfriends. So, given my obsession and everyone else's interest, I thought a lesbian relationship column might attract a following.

I also wanted to help level the political playing field here in Colorado Springs where homosexuals have been under siege by

Amendment 2, Colorado's anti-gay amendment. Since, in Colorado Springs, it seems that everything in print these days is anti-gay, I think homosexuality deserves some good press for a change.

Lesbians are in the closet in more ways than one. Despite the close friendships many of us seem to have, the self-help books we read, the therapy dollars we've spent, much of the *real truth* about our intimate relationships—the sorrow *and* the joy—remains hidden. Hidden even from our partners and ourselves, at times. The degree of isolation in much of the lesbian community, the "lies, secrets and silences" (to borrow a phrase from Adrienne Rich) makes me terribly sad. So one of the purposes of this column is to bring our relationship issues out of the closet so that we can normalize them. Another purpose for this column is to provide a forum in which to celebrate the miracle that is lesbian love.

All love is hard. Lesbian love is *harder*—given the toxic effects of discrimination, the ways in which our love is devalued, dismissed, and degraded, the rejection and harm we risk if we're honest about our love *or* the self-hatred and depression we risk if we conceal our love. Long-term lesbian relationships are not for the fainthearted. Many couples are out there struggling to make their relationships work under the worst of odds. They need acknowledgment, encouragement, and visibility. They also need *support*. I hope this column can offer support.

This column is also for me. Relationship fanatics need forums too. I want to be able to share the passion I feel for all of us who dare to love and be loved, and I especially want to share the passion I feel in my relationship with Maureen. So this column will be a further step in my own coming-out process as a lesbian *and* as a lover. This past September, I turned fifty. I think this column has something to do with that passage as well. I'm now beyond the reproductive years and, although I birthed the only child I ever wanted, I feel a profound sadness upon losing the reproductive option. I want to move through my menopausal years with consciousness and stay awake to the promise and possibilities of midlife. This column feels like part of that promise—a way of transforming my reproductive energy, a way of becoming an elder, a way of sharing my life stories. I'm also becoming a crone. From what

I've been told, crones get to say whatever we think, whenever we want, without ever being held liable!

A few disclaimers: although I am a seasoned psychotherapist, I want this column to speak more from my personal point of view, rather than from my clinical experience. I am not pretending to be a relationship expert. Frankly, I don't believe in such beings. I approach my own relationship with an incredible amount of humility, a "beginner's mind." Any suggestions I might venture to make are not necessarily what I'm practicing at home. This column, therefore, cannot be a replacement for your own good sense and/or professional help. And, you are hereby cautioned against using any of my words as ammunition in the next fight with your girlfriend.

So, start sending in your questions. I'll be composing my own until I hear from you.

In the meantime, don't ever forget, your love matters.

Being in the closet takes a terrible toll on your spirit. Every time you change pronouns or stifle a comment about your home life, you cause another micro-injury to your soul.

Susan Love
quoted in *The Lesbian News*

Sex Lives

My research shows that the frequency of sex among lesbian couples drops off dramatically after the first year, then keeps sinking, sort of like Beethoven's Fifth: Dah Dah Dah . . . Dum.

JoAnn Loulan
Lesbian Passion

"Dah Dah Dah . . . Dum." Does Beethoven's *Fifth* describe your sex life, now or in the past? I've read a couple of studies, but there are probably more than that. What I've read, and the experiences I hear, seem to indicate that lesbian couples have very passionate, very frequent sex when they first meet; but the frequency and passion wear off pretty early into the relationship. A study by Blumstein and Schwartz (as reported in *Lesbian Couples* [1988] by Clunis and Green) found that lesbian couples have sex less often than any other type of couple at every stage of their relationships. The Loulan study, as reported in her book *Lesbian Passion* (1987), surveyed 1,566 single and coupled lesbians. Although this study used a nonrandom approach and lacks generalized validity, it does indicate some definite patterns. In regard to frequency, the Loulan respondents said that in a typical month: 12 percent never have sex; 19 percent have sex once or fewer times; 35 percent, two to five times; 20 percent, six to ten times; and 14 percent, eleven or more times. For couples, the incidence of partner sex decreased, on the average, from ten to twelve times a month in the first year of a relationship to four to six times a month by the end of three years. These are the results from the lesbians who are *willing* to talk. What about those lesbians who are not talking? So, although many lesbians say they love sex and want it more often, it appears that their actual sex lives do not reflect their desires. What's going on?

First, let's take a look at that "honeymoon" period. That's the time in which we've recently become attracted and have decided that we like each other well enough to make love. And we do. And it's fantastic. Who can ever forget what "honeymoon sex" feels like? In that stage, we stay up all night getting to know each other and have sex. And have sex. And have sex. That's the period in which we are in such a daze that we miss work, forget to eat, dump all our friends. It's during the "honeymoon," we find ourselves saying such things as:

- I feel like I've known her my entire life.
- I've never felt so close to anyone before.
- It's the most extraordinary sex I've ever had.

These feelings are particularly true for lesbians. There is a special magic in lesbian love. An incredible bonding does take place. We merge. We feel completely connected. It's so sweet! And the sex is so compelling, we can think of nothing else. We are under, what I've affectionately coined, the mating spell. And it *is* a spell, a real phenomenon. It is not an illusion. It is a true biochemical high, a built-in evolutionary mechanism designed to compel us to have sex and to fall in love. The biochemical high overrides everything else: how we feel about ourselves, who our new partner really is, what the world thinks about us. And it is the high that creates the expectation that *this relationship really will be different*. Based on this expectation, we make a commitment to be together. These feelings can't lie, we think.

Only the high is not designed to *sustain* the relationship. It's only designed to *create* the relationship. Once we've mated, the high begins to dissolve. The sexual passion decreases. Other relationship demands surface. A different reality settles in. We argue more and make love less. Now we find ourselves saying:

- I feel like I don't even know her anymore.
- Sex has become so routine, so predictable, so boring . . .
- I love her, but I'm not sure I'm *in love* anymore.

Once a commitment is made, it seems as if our relationship changes dramatically. We've gotten to know each other well enough that our "little selves" emerge—the sad infant, the scared toddler, the rebellious teenager. We start hurting, disappointing, and resenting each other. Our differences surface. They intimidate us. We have difficulty accepting our partners or (even) ourselves. Our everyday realities distract and overwhelm us—work, money, health, family. We become blaming, disconnected, polarized. Our sex lives suffer.

And lesbian sex has unique hardships—secrecy, sexism, oppression. How can we sustain passion in the midst of wounded hearts, hiding, and hatefulness? . . . with great difficulty, if at all. These hardships affect how we feel about ourselves, how we feel about each other, how we feel about sex. After awhile, it becomes easier to be just the roommates that everyone wants us to be. For some couples, this loss of sex seems not to be a problem (at least that's what some women report). Other couples have found ways to keep their sex lives alive (write and tell us how). But most couples report that their sex lives have suffered and, at least one, if not both members of the couple, experience this loss as very significant and extremely painful. At this point, many lesbians break up or seek an affair . . . anything to get that magical feeling back.

So, what's called for here? Quick Fix? Easy answers? Twelve-step sexual recovery program? I don't think so. Anyone offering simple solutions is a liar. *There are no simple solutions.* Sex is a tangled web. How can something feel so good and be so difficult? But it is. It really is. And, if we start with the expectation that sex is hard and requires work (once the honeymoon is over), we'll have a good beginning to a difficult problem.

With sex and every other relationship issue, you are going to hear consistent advice from this column. *Be willing to do whatever work it takes* to stay connected to each other, despite the problem.

- Take 100 percent share of the responsibility.
- Increase your awareness.
- Change your expectations.

Then, and only then, do you have a working relationship.
  In the meantime, don't ever forget, your love matters.

Dumpling Girl

A southern dumpling child
   biscuit eater, tea sipper
   okra slicer, gravy dipper,
I fry my potatoes with onions
   stew my greens with pork

And ride my lover high up
on the butterfat shine of her thighs
where her belly arches and sweetly tastes
of rock salt on watermelon
sunshine sharp teeth bite light
and lick slow like mama's
favorite dumpling child.

Dorothy Allison
The Women Who Hate Me:
Poetry 1980-1990

Relationship Polarity

Question: My girlfriend, Tess, and I have a problem. Both of us were pretty closeted before Amendment 2. Since then, I've become very active in the gay and lesbian movement. That activity has really helped me feel better about who I am. Tess is shy, has trouble with her self-esteem, and remains pretty homophobic. I think she could really benefit from getting involved in the movement, as I have. I keep trying to find ways to persuade her, but the more I talk, the more she withdraws. The more she withdraws, the angrier I get. What do you think we should do?

Cindy, Out and Liking It

Answer: Your problem sounds like a classic example of what I call relationship polarity. Practically every relationship has its share:

- I want sex. She doesn't.
- She likes to eat out. I like to cook.
- I jog five miles a day. She's a couch potato.

In the beginning of a relationship, these differences don't seem to bother us. They might even excite us. Or, they might not have emerged yet. But as the relationship progresses, the differences cause conflicts, and polarization sets in. What are our options when relationship polarities occur?

Approach Number One

This is usually the first line of defense—the most comfortable and most familiar, the "I'll just try to change her" approach. Cindy and Tess seem to be stuck in this approach. Both partners will try this approach as often as they can get away with it, but they usually have different styles. There's the overt style, which Cindy seems to be using. She's directly telling Tess what's best for her. And there's the covert style. Tess is more covert, it seems—the "I'll just withdraw until she gets tired of asking me" approach. Whether its overt or covert, the goal is still the same. Let's see who can control this situation. Although this approach often has some short-term gains, in the long run, it's a relationship Dead End. Before you know it, Tess will withdraw right out the front door with her suitcase in hand.

Approach Number Two

When persuasion, pleading, and ultimatums don't work, many couples will turn to compromise or negotiation. "Okay," says Cindy, "if you agree to come to at least one Ground Zero meeting, I'll agree to clean the house for the next five years." Or, "I've got an idea," says Tess, "you get off my back about this, and I'll do your laundry for the rest of my life." Now some relationship differences might really lend themselves to approach number two: for instance, if you're fighting about which restaurant to eat in tonight, which TV show to watch, which vacation to take. Compromise, negotiation, even capitulation can work when neither partner is required to give up or lose what she feels to be a vital part of herself. Tess and Cindy's problem, however, does not appear to fall into this category. They both seem to have too much to lose here.

Approach Number Three

This approach is designed for struggles in which one, if not both partners, feel that *their very survival is at stake*. By survival, I mean a *perceived* sense of *loss of love* and/or *loss of self*. True or imagined, such losses might feel life threatening—like you really might die. Survival issues are often at the root of relationship struggles. They are what make us feel so entrenched in our positions.

I wonder whether survival issues aren't at the bottom of Tess and Cindy's problems. For instance, it sounds as if Tess feels very threatened by the idea of coming out. Does Tess fear rejection by her parents? Loss of job? Fear about physical safety? Does Tess fear loss of self if she gives in to Cindy's demands? And what about Cindy's survival issues? She sounds pretty threatened, too. Could Cindy fear the loss of Tess's love now that their interests are in conflict? Does Cindy feel scared and alone out there in the world without Tess? How safe does Cindy feel now that she is out of the closet? Is she as comfortable as she professes? I don't know. I'm only guessing.

What I do know is that this kind of relationship polarity calls for great understanding, compassion, and acceptance of each other. It presents a challenge and an opportunity to more deeply connect to each other through getting in touch with the *feelings* that underlie the positions and the polarity. Herein lies one of the greatest relationship tools—a genuine willingness to know yourself and your partner on a deeper level. If I were Cindy, I would want to know what Tess is afraid of losing. Is she really afraid of coming out and, if so, why? Is Tess afraid of losing herself to Cindy, and what would make her afraid of that? Is it true that Tess is shy and her self-esteem is low? If true, how did that happen? If I were Tess, I would want to know why this issue is so important to Cindy. What was keeping Cindy in the closet *before* Amendment 2? Why is it that Cindy feels better about herself now that she is out? What does it feel like for Cindy to be in the movement without her partner? How confident is Cindy in Tess's love? What does Cindy feel she would gain by Tess's involvement? What is it that Cindy is afraid of losing?

So, my advice to Tess and Cindy: Don't resist the polarity, embrace it. Your relationship struggle is ripe with opportunity. You can choose to use this difference to polarize and misalign or you can choose to use this difference to deepen your connection and realign. Which will it be?

And how about the rest of you out there? How are you choosing to use the polarities in your relationships?

In the meantime, don't ever forget, your love matters.

To enter into an intimate relationship is to be swept up in a play of self and other, a ceaseless dance of shifting polarities.

John Welwood
Journey of the Heart:
Intimate Relationships and the Path of Love

Finances

Question: How should lesbian couples handle their finances? What happens when one person earns a lot more than the other? What do you think is fair, right, and effective?

Melissa

Answer: A money question. Wow! First, I was really excited to receive a question, any question. Then I was really excited to respond to a question about money and lesbians, since money is such a taboo subject (more taboo than sex if you can believe that). But once I started thinking and writing on the subject, I got really stuck. I didn't have any ready-made answers. I had a lot of muddled thoughts and conflicted feelings. Writing this column is forcing me to try to come to terms with a topic I would rather keep in the closet as do many of my lesbian sisters. So, to the writer who asked this question: Thanks for "outing" me on this difficult subject.

In heterosexual marriages, there are underlying assumptions and established rules for the management of money. These assumptions are supported in law. Although some married couples may choose to deviate from the norm, at least they have a cultural standard by which to formulate and measure their financial agreements. This is not so in the lesbian subculture. For us, no underlying assumptions or established rules exist. There are no protocols, no laws, no prescribed roles, no rituals. We probably do not even have any mentors or guides to look to for advice and counsel. We feel alone, isolated and confused. We're really starting from scratch. In the beginning, that may feel liberating. After all, we are free to design a system without any constraints. But once we get into the process, it might begin to feel overwhelming. How do we proceed in the absence of any standards or roadmaps? What is fair? What is right? What does work?

Do we know very much about the financial arrangements of lesbian couples? Actually, the topic has been researched and written about to some degree. Blumstein and Schwartz speak extensively about money and lesbians in their research study book, *American Couples: Money, Work, Sex* (1983). Susan Johnson discusses money in her study of lesbian couples, *Staying Power: Long-Term Lesbian Couples* (1991). Betty Berzon devotes a chapter to "Money Issues" in her book, *Permanent Partners* (1988). What have the experts found out? Well, there seems to be a great deal of diversity in our financial arrangements. Most of these arrangements, however, can be organized along a continuum. On one end of the continuum lie those couples who most resemble heterosexual marriages. That is, they commingle all or most of their income and assets. They own a home together or are joint tenants on a lease. Their checking and savings accounts are joint as are their spending decisions. Each knows exactly how much the other earns, spends, and saves. They have definite rules and rituals regarding the bills and the books. These couples think of themselves as a single financial unit. On the other end of the continuum lie those couples who do not commingle their finances at all. They most resemble heterosexual cohabitating couples. These couples do not co-own a home, a car, or a stick of furniture, whether or not they live together. They maintain separate bank accounts, make independent decisions about all their spending, and may not even know exactly how much each earns, saves, or spends. These couples think of themselves as two distinct financial units. In the middle of the continuum lie the rest of lesbian couples. Perhaps this is where the average couple resides. These couples maintain some combination of pooling and separating their resources. They might have purchased a home together. They probably maintain a joint "household" account. Their vehicles are probably separate as are their savings accounts. They probably jointly own some furniture or kitchen equipment, maybe even a house on the Riviera! They probably know a lot about each other's finances, but not everything. They contribute toward the joint expenses in either an equal or proportional way, dependent upon respective income and values. These couples think of their resources as yours, mine, and ours. Wherever we fall along this continuum, you can be sure we have devised some unique and idiosyncratic practices. Very few lesbian financial arrangements look exactly the same.

What factors are influencing the choices we make about how to handle our money? Many. For instance: *Trust and commitment:* How well do we trust each other? To what degree do we believe that this relationship will last? How committed are we to a permanent relationship? How safe do we feel with intimacy, interdependence? *Values and histories:* What are our values regarding earning, managing, and spending money? What history are these values based in? Do we enjoy spending money or hoarding it? Do we earn, spend, and save money according to a budget? Or are we spontaneous? Do we see money as abundant or scarce? Did we grow up rich or poor? *Homophobia:* Are we out to our families, our employers, our bankers, our financial managers? Is our financial arrangement based on how comfortable or uncomfortable we feel being out? *Power and control:* To what degree is money used to maintain power and control? What is the balance of power in the relationship? Is there fear that there will be a power and control imbalance if money is pooled, if money is kept separate? *Practicality, convenience, and particular circumstances:* How much money does each partner have? How did she get it? Is a particular financial arrangement just plain practical or convenient? Given the facts, is it just easier to manage money one way or another? Are there children or other dependent persons involved? Are there unique circumstances that dictate the financial system that is used? Many factors and issues determine our choices. Lots of confusion.

But is there a right or wrong way to handle our finances? What is politically correct? Is one way more effective than another? What *do* the experts say? There actually seems to be some consensus among the experts. That doesn't make them right, of course, but here's some of what they have to say. The Johnson study researched 108 lesbian couples who had been together for at least ten years (24 percent of whom had been together for twenty years or more). Johnson found that 55 percent of these couples share *all* their money and 70 percent pool their money to some significant degree. Blumstein and Schwartz found a high correlation between the permanence in lesbian relationships and the willingness to pool finances. They also found that the longer lesbian couples lived together, the more they tended to pool their financial resources. Betty Berzon states, "The merging of the couple's money is an expression of their commitment to each other and to the relationship" (p. 262).

These experts seem to agree on two major points. The first is that lesbian relationships are very fragile. Blumstein and Schwartz found, to their surprise (and mine), that lesbian couples have the highest breakup rate of all American couples they surveyed— including married couples, heterosexual cohabitors, and gay men. The second point is that financial interdependence is a stabilizing force in lesbian relationships. Thus, their data support the arguments for pooling resources. Is that what I am recommending? Is that what I practice within my own relationship?

I certainly see the instability in lesbian relationships. It's a source of pain and sorrow to me. I also see the need for anchoring relationships which often seem afloat. Combining financial resources is most definitely one way of stabilizing our relationships. Although Maureen and I feel very anchored in our soon-to-be fourteen-year relationship, we still maintain a high degree of financial independence. While there's been a definite trend toward pooling, (especially in the second half of our relationship), we still haven't had a need or desire to completely combine our resources. What we have discovered a need and desire for, however, is much more conversation on the subject of money and much more definition to our "financial system." Our "system" has developed over time in a haphazard way. We're not sure exactly how we got here or what "here" actually is. So our financial relationship is definitely a work in progress.

The anchors we are cultivating in our relationship are more about process than any particular outcome. That is, with money and all other issues, we are more concerned with *how* we arrive at a decision than the decision itself. Both of us seem able to adapt to any number of relationship decisions if we feel that our process is a conscious and collaborative one. By that we mean a process in which both of us have had the time and opportunity to explore our thoughts and feelings on the issue and convey those thoughts and feelings in a way in which we feel heard, understood, and respected. Having done that, we are ready to make a decision—if that seems appropriate. We evaluate our relationship process by the degree to which each of us now feels safe and satisfied with the outcome. So whether we decide to pool money or not, if both of us feel good about our process, then we feel connected. When we feel connected, we feel anchored.

I hope my thoughts can be of help to all of you struggling with a complex and confusing subject.

In the meantime, don't ever forget, your love matters.

Money establishes the balance of power in relationships, except among lesbians.

Philip Blumstein
Pepper Schwartz
American Couples: Money, Work, Sex

Breakup Rates

Question: You stated in your column that lesbian relationships are least likely to last in comparison to gay men and hetero-sexuals. Did the study say why?

Just Wondering

Answer: Why? It's a million-dollar question in the lesbian community, isn't it? Every day in my office and in my friendship circle, I hear stories about lesbian breakups. I think it's the number one issue that brings lesbians into therapy with me. In my own friendship circle, last year alone, three couples close to my heart broke up. It was devastating to all of us.

Despite wanting to talk about this subject with my readers, I have had some serious resistance. The resistance has to do with all the pain that comes up when we begin talking about our losses. In addition, whenever relationships *do* end, we have a tendency to go beyond the necessary self-examination to a place of "blame" and "shame." We begin thinking of ourselves as "bad" or "sick." I do not want to say anything that would contribute to these feelings. My purpose in writing about this subject is to deepen our understanding about lesbian coupling and to do so in a way in which we feel cared for and supported. I hope I can do that.

The study referred to was conducted by Philip Blumstein and Pepper Schwartz. The results were published in 1983 in a book titled *American Couples: Money, Work, Sex*. This study attracted my attention because the authors went to great lengths to include lesbians and gays in their research and did so in a "gay-friendly" way. Although the study may well be outdated by now (and may even have some methodological flaws), I am finding the results helpful to me as I examine the ups and downs of lesbian relationships.

The purpose of the research was to study the lives of four kinds of American couples (married, heterosexual-cohabitating, gays, lesbians) particularly in regard to money, work, and sex. Extensive questionnaires and in-depth interviews were utilized. The sample included 772 lesbian couples and 957 gay couples. One of the dimensions studied was "breakup rates." To establish these rates, approximately half of all the couples originally surveyed were resurveyed eighteen months later to see how many had broken up and why. The authors were surprised to find that lesbians had the highest breakup rate in their study. Although they could not explain this finding with any certainty, they did have some theories. I will share just a couple of them with you.

Blumstein and Schwartz found that lesbians have a number of conflicting desires in their relationships, particularly about their female roles. Although there are many aspects of the female role that lesbians find demeaning, we embrace other aspects of being female. Lesbians want to avoid being dependent or having a dependent partner. We want to avoid dominating or being dominated. We do not want to be the provider nor do we wish to be provided for. We want strong, ambitious, and independent partners. However, lesbians also want very strong, intense home lives. We want a great deal of attention and communication from our partners. We want our relationships to be placed at the center of our lives. We have a high need for emotional intensity. These needs and desires are exceptionally challenging and often in conflict. We are actually trying to carve out a new female role. This challenge puts a unique stress on our relationships.

It definitely puts stress on mine. In the absence of traditional gender directives, for instance, Maureen and I use a trial-and-error approach to establishing roles and assigning tasks. In the beginning of our relationship, it seemed a liberating idea to redefine ourselves and structure our relationship outside of tradition and convention. But it is also a huge responsibility. We often find ourselves in a double bind. On the one hand, we reject the patriarchal way of relating as too oppressive. On the other hand, we wish someone would just tell us what to do. Our needs and desires are often in conflict. As much as we value our independence and autonomy, there are many moments in which each of us longs to be taken care of.

A second challenge for lesbian couples identified in this study concerned romantic expectations. Since *all* women prize romance, their transitions from the early euphoria of relationships to the routines of everyday life will be difficult. The transition for lesbians, this study suggests, may be all the more troubling because there are *two* women in the relationship longing for the way it used to feel. Lesbian couples often lack anchors (like children or businesses), and the temptation to go outside the relationship to regain the early excitement is very high. Blumstein and Schwartz say that "lesbians are often in tight-knit friendship groups where friends and acquaintances spend so much intimate time together, that . . . , opportunities arise for . . . love and a meaningful affair" (p. 322). That's an all-too-familiar scenario in the lives of lesbians, isn't it?

I think the issue goes beyond "romance," although I do think that lesbians are hopelessly romantic. I think I bring enormous emotional expectations to my lesbian relationship—expectations that go beyond what is reasonable and appropriate. I call these expectations "Looking for the Perfect Mommy" syndrome. In my relationship, there's a part of me that is not just looking for a reasonably good partner to love, comfort and hold me, to accept me for who I am. I'm not just wanting an "occasional" mommy to comfort my tender, sensitive, broken heart. I want The Perfect Mommy, available on a twenty-four-hour basis, whose job it is, not only to take care of me, but to *save* me, heal me, and make me whole again. As much as I'd like to deny needing such a mommy in my rational, adult space, I have come to understand that this is really what my little unconscious mind craves.

In lesbian relationships, it's easy to get fooled. Our partner is a woman. She has a mommy's heart. She has a mommy's body. She is truly a mommy persona. On a very primal level, our deepest needs for our real mothers get stimulated. That is, in fact, part of what makes our initial connection so hot. While there is, at least initially, that magical connection, and while our girlfriends can sometimes act like very good mommy substitutes, the truth is still the same. That is, we're never *really* going to get those old mommy needs met. Never. Our lovers, in the moment, can mother us. But they cannot *be* our mothers. The pain that comes up, given that loss, is devastating and enraging. We are sorely tempted to label that pain a "defective partner." If we aren't conscious of what is really happening on an emotional level and don't find a way of addressing the pain from an internal point of view, we will externalize it. We will start looking for another perfect mommy. In lesbian communities, another mommy persona is right around the next corner.

I'm interested in what my readers think. This is just a "theory in progress." I certainly see this theory operating in my own relationship. When my primal mommy needs come up, I find them extremely confusing. I truly believe they are about *this* relationship. When my girlfriend can't meet those needs, I think she is trying to torture me. I want to kill her or dump her! But then I do the emotional work that I've learned to do (to get in touch with where the pain and the needs are actually coming from), and I work on it at its core. I then feel much better, and my girlfriend becomes the wonderful partner I know her to be.

These are some of the special challenges of lesbian relationships. I wouldn't trade them for the world! Let me know what you think about all this. Keep your letters coming.

In the meantime, don't ever forget, your love matters.

Love Is Not One of Those Countries
Where You Can Be Sure of the Weather

the storm that broke last weekend
over Brittany where you were
staying with another woman
the gale that wrecked ships
the rain that flooded towns
and washed them out to sea
that torrent in the west
that howl of pain
was me
wanting you back
wishing you drowned
watching hope drip out of me like blood
declaring myself a disaster area

Jacqueline Lapidus
Starting Over

Menopause

Question: I'm fifty-two and my partner, Sandy, is forty. I'm well into menopause and have been noticing some sexual changes that are bothersome. My vagina is quite dry and irritated, my desire level has declined, and I'm not as easily orgasmic as I'm used to being. Sandy and I have been together for fifteen years and have both really enjoyed our sex life. I'm sad about these changes, and Sandy feels threatened. She's afraid I've lost my desire for her. Do you have any ideas about how we can handle these changes?

Mary

Answer: I'm fifty and have been going through menopause for the last several years, as well, and can share with you some of the ways in which I've been handling these changes. First, let me say that menopause has been one of the most profound life experiences I've ever had, on every level—physical, emotional, and spiritual. I really hadn't known what to expect. My mom's experience hadn't seemed extraordinary, and I really hadn't heard or listened to the experiences of other women before my own process began. It's important not to go through this experience alone or isolated. My first recommendation, therefore, is to:

Gather Information and Support

Information has been incredibly reassuring to me as I maneuver menopause. I needed to know what was happening to my body, to my heart, and to my spirit. Like Mary, I noticed many changes in sexual interest and responsiveness. At first, it seemed sad and scary to me and to Maureen. Once I began to understand what my body was actually going through, and I was able to convey that knowledge to Maureen, many of our feelings became more manageable.

For instance, I learned that many menopausal women report changes in their sexuality. As estrogen levels decline, there are differences in vaginal lubrication. We produce less lubrication; lubrication is thinner; lubrication takes longer to produce. The vaginal lining gets thinner and loses some elasticity. Pelvic tissue is generally less resilient. These changes can compromise our sexual comfort and responsiveness. Along with a decline in estrogen, many women may experience a loss of testosterone. Since testosterone is primarily responsible for sexual drive, desire and arousal capacity are also affected. Lowered testosterone decreases clitoral sensation, which results in less intense and/or less frequent orgasms. The combined effects of lowered estrogen and testosterone (as well as the ratios between and among all of our reproductive hormones) can lead to a significantly altered sexual experience. While this is not true of *all* menopausal women (a minority actually experience enhanced sexual pleasure), it does seem to be the experience for a majority of us. Such information can help explain why Mary's sexual responsiveness is changing. This information has the potential to help Sandy frame these changes in a less threatening and less personal way.

Although Mary's problem sounds primarily physical, other factors could be affecting her sexuality and should be checked out. Is Mary taking any drugs that might be altering her sexual experience—antidepressants, diuretics, antihistamines, or decongestants? Does she use alcohol? How often? How does she feel about aging? Are any other menopausal symptoms affecting lovemaking—fatigue, hot flashes, insomnia, joint pain?

What kind of support does Mary have? I've needed to gather a "support team" to assist me in the menopause process—a network of helpers to support my body, heart, and spirit through these changes. My team has included, at any given time, other menopausal women, a gynecologic nurse practitioner, a massage therapist, a chiropractor, a psychotherapist. All these helpers have some expertise in menopause and special interest in lesbian concerns. They've provided information, understanding, support, and a safe place to go and actually talk about what's happening to me. My "support team" has helped me sort out conflicting medical advice and helped me design a treatment plan tailored to my unique needs. For instance, I'm using a vaginal cream that has really helped with the dryness and irritation.

I'm using Progest (a wild yam cream) and a host of vitamins and herbs to treat my symptoms. My sexuality is enhanced by regular exercise and a healthy diet. Kegel (pelvic muscle) exercises have improved my sexual muscle tone. Many of these approaches have been suggested by members of my support team. I highly recommend that both Mary and Sandy cultivate a support system to help them through this change of life.

Communicate About Feelings

Communication between Mary and Sandy is the most effective "treatment" for these problems. Although some medical remedies and treatments are available to assist with the sexual symptoms, nothing is as powerful as talking about what each of them is thinking, feeling, and needing. Communication has been the most helpful strategy for me and Maureen. I needed to share my sadness about the sexual changes as well as my fears about Maureen feeling rejected. I needed to describe how my sexual experience was altered. I wanted Maureen to know that my needs were changing and how they were changing. Maureen needed to share her feelings, as well—what it was she was missing, how the experience was altered for her, what emerging needs she had. We both needed a lot of reassurance that we still loved each other, desired each other, and were committed to finding ways of keeping our sex life satisfying even though it was changing. This level of communication enabled us to stay connected and aligned through these menopausal changes.

Experiment with Your Lovemaking Strategies

Once Maureen and I realized that changes in my sexual responsiveness were normal and natural, we became willing to be creative, inventive, and experimental in our lovemaking strategies. The old ways (which had worked for so many years) were just not working anymore. We had to go back to the drawing board. Specifically, we needed to prolong our lovemaking, pace ourselves differently. We needed to look at the touch we were using and modify it to some degree. We needed to change where and when we made love. We found some new sexual aids, and we discovered a wonderful way to supplement lubrication with an over-the-counter lubricant called "Astroglide." We highly recommend it. It can be found in most pharmacies where condoms are sold. During lovemaking, place a *small* amount of Astroglide in and around your vagina (as well as directly on your clitoris). Astroglide feels very similar to natural lubrication and really enhances arousal.

Give Thanks for Being a Lesbian

Some positive research findings: According to Ellen Cole and Esther Rothblum, lesbian women have an easier time adapting to the sexual changes they experience during menopause. This research is reported in the chapter titled "Lesbian Sex at Menopause: as Good as or Better Than Ever" found in the wonderful anthology *Lesbians at Midlife: The Creative Transition* (1991). According to Ellen Cole, in the February 1995 issue of *A Friend Indeed* (Vol. IX, No. 9)

> . . . the lesbians I've surveyed and interviewed do seem, in general to have a positive attitude about menopause and aging. They do seem to be less subject than heterosexual women to the wrath of ageism and partner expectations. They do not seem to descend so deeply into ageist and sexist despair, even when the issues . . . are the same. (pp. 1-3)

So give thanks for being a menopausal lesbian. How many men could you find who would be willing to rub yam cream on your tummy, smear Astroglide on your clitoris, and do Kegel exercises together?

In the meantime, don't ever forget, your love matters.

Menopause is the invisible experience. People don't want to hear about it. But this is the time when everything comes good for you—your humor, your style, your bad temper.

Germaine Greer
The Change: Women, Aging, and the Menopause

I love playing hooky from my period.

Maureen Stevens
January 1998

Long-Distance Relationships

Question: Why is it that I find long-distance relationships much easier to deal with than when a lover's in the same house, city, or state? . . . My current lover and I spend one weekend per month together. We talk on the phone twice a week. Our jobs revolve around people, so neither of us actually minds the quiet time in the evening—our pets keep us occupied. I've had three long-distance relationships lasting between two and six years. What I miss most is "bumping butts" in the night and talking about the day's events, be they negative or positive.

Sally

Answer: Without knowing more about Sally, the family she grew up in, the intimacy models she saw, her attachments and losses, etc., I can't really speculate on her particular situation. It seems as if parts of her feel very safe in long-distance relationships and parts of her feel lonely and sad. For now, it seems that the larger part of her must need things to stay as they are.

There are, however, a number of ways in which I can relate to Sally's situation. To a large degree, I believe each of us comes into the world with open arms and an open heart, ready to embrace love. But because being human is so terribly difficult, our little hearts get broken over time—by our parents, our siblings, our teachers, and our friends. We get forgotten, overlooked, misunderstood, hurt, and ignored. Our hearts get broken in a million different ways. At times, our childhood pain is so great, it truly feels as if we are going to die. To protect ourselves, to survive, we learn to guard our hearts. We learn to keep love at a distance. In our own unique, idiosyncratic, and brilliant ways, we invent a set of distancing strategies. Despite how much we need to be loved, we also know how much love can hurt. So we attempt to mediate this conflict by seeking love—but keeping it at a safe distance.

Geographic distance can be a very effective strategy. Although lonely at times, it leaves one feeling safe enough to continue experiencing love as exciting and desirable. I had a long-distance lover once when I was in the seventh grade. He lived in New York. I lived in Baltimore. He was a dream—handsome, funny, sexy, and head over heels in love with me. We saw each other rarely but wrote letters constantly and longed for the time we could REALLY BE with one another. My girlfriends were totally jealous. What they didn't know was that he was a dream in more ways than one. I had made him up; he was fiction. I had desperately wanted to be in love. I wanted my friends to think I was in love. But I was too young, too afraid, too vulnerable to really be in love. That distancing strategy was incredibly effective.

Soon after, I began falling in love with actual people. And then the real work began. As often as I fell in love and as much as I believed I was ready for it, my broken heart kept getting in the way. I devised a number of distancing strategies. Overzealous participation in politics. Workaholism. Rage. Triangles. Judgment. Withdrawal. Polygamy. Positioning. You name it, I tried it. As years went by, my armor got thicker. By the time I hit my mid-thirties, I had enough armor for a world war. The trouble was that I was so well protected, I scarcely had feelings *myself*, let alone feelings about anyone else. Nothing much was getting in. I felt pretty depressed, pretty numb, pretty incapable of any kind of love. At that time, I went into therapy, examined my worn-out distancing strategies, and decided to address my broken heart in new and different ways.

I guess what I'm saying here is that the closer we get to those we love, the more dangerous love begins to feel. For every human being, there is a fine line between seeing your partner as your Beloved, and seeing your partner as the Enemy. While bumping butts in the night can feel tender, passionate, and cozy, there are also many times in which it's going to feel lethal. Each of us has to find a way to love that not only nurtures us but protects us. For Sally, that might mean a long-distance relationship. I don't know. What I do know, however, is that the work that is required to sustain a day-to-day, live-together, close and connected relationship is harder than most of us can even imagine.

So, Sally, enjoy and appreciate the love that you do have in your current long-distance relationship and take heart from some tender words of Stephen Levine from his book, *Healing into Life and Death* (1987): "even a millisecond of love is a miracle" (p. 69).

In the meantime, don't ever forget, your love matters.

Living Together

we agree we do not own
each other   there is space
for her where I live

I clear old lovers off the shelves
carefully she unpacks her habits,
spoons confidence into cups

I open myself like a window
she breathes deeply
we get high on each other's skin

houseproud, we forget the building's
old and shaky   we ignore
the rain, the leaking roof

like paint our promises begin
to blister   the ceiling cracks
suspicion seeps through the wall

can we cover it with plaster? how
can we be sure it will not
fall on us while we sleep?

Jacqueline Lapidus
Starting Over

Dating

There are two possible outcomes of a lesbian date; either the two women never date again, or they get married.

JoAnn Loulan
Lesbian Passion

Question: Why do lesbians find it so hard to date? By dating, I mean spending a good deal of time getting to know each other before calling it a relationship and/or getting to know a number of different people before zeroing in on one. It would seem to save a great deal of grief later on if we really knew who we were marrying.

Dateless in Denver

Answer: Dating is a topic about which I can only speculate. I don't have much experience doing it. My only experience is in avoiding it. All the relationship experts seem to be suggesting it. I certainly have. The conventional wisdom is that lesbians could have longer lasting, higher quality relationships if they shopped around first. Makes sense on paper. In real life, however, dating seems to strike terror in the hearts of most lesbians. Why is that?

Actually, I think dating is terrifying for most human beings: gay, straight, female, male. It feels as if we're really putting ourselves on the line to date—especially when we contemplate initiating a date. Many of us say we feel too vulnerable to initiate a date. Others say it feels too awkward, unnatural. Dating brings up all of our self-esteem issues. Are we good enough, smart enough, cute enough? As much as we long to be loved, we are terrified to put ourselves out there for fear no one will ever choose us. We are deathly afraid of rejection. If we don't ask, we can't be refused. We're also afraid of acceptance. What if we ask and the answer is yes? Can we really handle that? As girls, we were taught to be sexually passive. As females, we seem to be naturally cautious. So, some of us just wait—hoping that if we go out to a party, to a bar, to a political gathering—and *look* available, maybe someone will just notice us.

We wait awhile to see if we meet anyone. Sometimes it happens right away. Sometimes it takes forever. Finally, someone does come along. We go out once or twice. She seems to really like you. You kind of like her back. She likes you enough to want to be in a relationship. Fearful that no one else will come along, flattered that someone really wants you, you decide to want her back. You begin a relationship.

Or, someone comes along whom you really want. She really wants you too. You've both recently had your hearts broken. You jump right into a relationship before either of you changes her mind. So much for taking some time. So much for playing the field. Our great emotional need to be loved keeps us from exploring the relationship potential. Our urgency concerning this need keeps us from dating more than one person at a time.

Our urgency is also driven by our evolutionary makeup. We are, after all, designed to fall in love, have sex, and reproduce. Once we are attracted to a person, we are under the influence of very powerful sexual chemicals. Whether we are planning on reproducing or not, these chemicals are compelling us to "mate." They put us in an altered state of consciousness in which we feel open, safe, euphoric, and complete. We feel as if we already know this person very deeply. We are convinced that *this is it*. We then lock into our new love. We make a commitment, confident that we have enough information. Looking any further is out of the question. Dating, after all, is a pretty rational activity. Mating is not.

As lesbians, dating offers some unique challenges. As someone I know said recently, "There are no social rules for lesbian dating like there are for other social activities, like asking a friend for dinner. So when I'm interested in someone, I just ask her if she wants to go to dinner." As a result, the friend probably doesn't know that she's being asked out on a date. Lots of lesbians tell me they're hanging out with someone new, but they are not exactly sure what it means. I've also heard some lesbians say they are attracted to someone new but they don't know for sure if the new person is a lesbian, and they are too afraid to ask.

Instead of being direct with a potential date, we pump our friends for information. "Is so and so a lesbian?" "Is she involved with anyone?" "Do you think she would be interested in me?" Asking her ourselves seems out of the question. And if we were so inclined as to ask, we don't know what to say. How do you ask a lesbian out on a date, anyway? How do you find out for sure if she is a lesbian or not? How do you distinguish dinner from a date? Many lesbians really struggle with these questions. None of us ever took a class in lesbian dating. Our moms didn't give us any tips. How's a lesbian supposed to know how to date?

Lesbians have another big problem—internal homophobia. Asking a lesbian for a date could arouse suspicion that I, myself, (horrors), might be of a similar persuasion. Many lesbians are too uncomfortable with their sexuality to spend much time dating or to be very direct in their dating. You see, each time we think about approaching another woman for a date, we come up against our lesbian self-esteem issues—those issues that Loulan (1987) calls our "lesbian snot" (p. 33). "It's the feeling that there is something wrong with being a lesbian. We all have it. Why else aren't we shouting our love from the rooftops?" (p. 33). Most of the time we keep our lesbian snot at bay. We fool ourselves into thinking we are perfectly comfortable with our sexuality. (After all, we were rarely having sex at the end of our last relationship.) Or, we try to pretend that we're not really lesbians. (Our last two relationships just happened to be with women.) Those kinds of rationalizations work fine most of the time—until we begin feeling lonely and start looking around for someone new to be with. Then we come face to face with our lesbian snot.

No wonder lesbians get married on the first date. Just making it to the first date is an act of courage. In order to date, lesbians must confront and override fear, homophobia, and hormones. So, while dating seems like such a sensible, grown-up, civilized alternative to getting married on the first date, it turns out to be quite the challenge, indeed.

I'm sure that there are many lesbians out there with successful dating experiences. Write to *Love Matters* and tell us how you do it.

Whether you're an expert or a novice at dating, you'll enjoy reading Loulan's (1987) chapter "The Lesbian Date."

In the meantime, don't ever forget, your love matters.

Fragment of a Night

That curved carved mouth,
That tender much-inventing wandering mouth!
I could say more. But now my lips are sealed.

Naomi Replansky
The Dangerous World

Forty Secrets
for a Happy Relationship

Question: *What's the secret to your successful fourteen-year relationship with Maureen?*

Suspicious

Answer:

1. Availability	21. Kindness
2. Awareness	22. Love
3. Hard Work	23. Magic
4. Commitment	24. Therapy and Hard Work
5. Compassion	25. Mercy
6. Connection	26. Open-heartedness
7. Therapy	27. Passion
8. Consciousness	28. Passion
9. Lots of Therapy	29. Passion
10. Courage	30. Lots of Hard Work
11. Devotion	31. Patience
12. Lots of Hard Work	32. Surrender
13. Faith	33. Therapy
14. Fidelity	34. Tenderness
15. Generosity	35. Therapy
16. Therapy	36. Truth
17. Gentleness	37. Truth
18. Lots of Hard Work	38. Vulnerability
19. Humility	39. Willingness
20. Humor	40. Therapy and Hard Work

In the meantime, don't ever forget, your love matters.

Speak your love
Speak it again
Speak it still once again

Anonymous

The Right Person

Question: How do I know whether or not I'm in a relationship with the RIGHT PERSON?

Unsigned

Answer: This is a question that all of us have asked ourselves at least once, if not many times, in our relationship lives. This is a very important question and is deserving of a number of different responses. I will write more than one column about it. While I was debating the kind of answer I would give, a very personal response emerged. It comes by way of an intimate story, which explains how I know I'm in a relationship with the right person.

I woke up recently in a very deep depression, an existential angst. I felt lost, alone, empty, sad, and scared. It felt as if, at least in that moment, I truly had forgotten who I was, what I was supposed to be doing, where I was supposed to be. I had awakened before Maureen and had gone into the living room—where I often sit, write, or think in the early morning—with a cup of coffee by my side. I began to cry a little, but it felt too scary to really let go. When I knew the alarm had gone off, I went back into the bedroom and lay beside Maureen. Before long, I really began crying. After I exhausted my tears, Maureen asked me to tell her how I was feeling, what was happening. I explained how disconnected I felt from myself, how lost I was. I said it felt like I needed someone to take me by the hand and show me the way again, to tell me who I was. As I shared with Maureen the depth and breadth of my feelings, she began to cry as well, as she often does when I share my pain. She was also able to ask questions and share similar feelings without taking charge in any way, without trying to make it go away, fix it, or tell me what to do. What she did was simply *be with me in the moment*, let me know how much she felt my pain, how much she cared for and about me. She was also able to tell me what it was about me that she loved, those characteristics of mine she treasured—including my angst. It felt as if the softest blanket in the world had wrapped around me—comforting and containing the pain. While Maureen wasn't able (nor would anyone else be) to take my pain away, she nourished my psyche and soul with her extraordinary emotional presence until I was ready to take my own hand and lead myself out of the darkness.

In that moment, and in many others like it, I know I am with the right person. Before Maureen, I had never been in a relationship in which I felt safe to be myself—to become all of who I really am. Maureen has that capacity to let me BE. When I feel strong, she is not threatened. When I feel vulnerable, she is not threatened. When I feel independent, she is not threatened. When I feel needy, she is not threatened. With that safety and support, I am finding my way to MYSELF.

Feeling safe to be myself is one of the most important ways in which I measure the "rightness" of my relationship with my partner. It took me a long time in life to identify the importance of that need, however. While I cannot pretend to feel safe every minute of my relationship, I can say that my relationship feels safe, *enough* of the time.

There are other important ways in which I measure the "rightness" of my partner and my relationship, and I will continue to write about those. For now I have to say that the emotional safety in my relationship is at the heart of its success.

In the meantime, don't ever forget, your love matters.

Compassion and love are precious things in life.
They are not complicated.
They are simple, but difficult to practice.

Dalai Lama
Tibetan Portrait

How to Keep Love Alive

Question: An acquaintance of mine is in the throes of a new relationship. Her descriptions go something like this: "It has never been like this before;" "What has been best is that we became friends first before becoming lovers." "We can talk about anything and tell each other everything we are feeling and thinking;" "Sex has never been like this before;" etc., etc. I remember thinking the same things at the beginning of my last partnership. Now it's over, and she lives over 1,000 miles away from me. How does one keep the same or similar passion, honesty, openness, and love alive for the duration?

J. D.

Answer: How much time do you have? You've asked a question that's bigger than life—so deep and complex. How can couples keep their love alive for the duration? While there's no way I can begin to answer that question for you or for anyone else, I can share a personal story about my life with Maureen. Perhaps within this story, you can find some meaning for your own life.

A couple of weeks ago, Maureen went on a golfing trip with her family. She was gone only a few days. Although I'm always very anxious right before she leaves, I usually look forward to the time alone. I devoted this time to a number of tasks—including my dreaded taxes. Somehow it seems easier for me to accomplish tasks like these when no one else is around. Time has a way of feeling more expansive when I'm alone—no one else to relate to, be distracted by, use up any energy on. I like it. The couple of weeks before Maureen left had been stressful for me. I was having some challenges with my body. My emotions were pretty raw. I had looked forward to the time alone for some personal caretaking and healing. Maureen left on a Wednesday with plans to return on Sunday evening. My time alone went as planned. I accomplished what I set out to accomplish—that is, I did my taxes, had some good alone time thinking and writing, and spent some satisfying time with friends. Maureen was having a grand old time herself, as she always does with her family (imagine that). We kept in touch by phone.

By the time Sunday rolled around, I was really looking forward to seeing Maureen. She's such a good friend, as well as my life partner, and I always miss her when she's gone. She's definitely one of my favorite people to talk to and hang out with. So when I got into my car Sunday night to drive to the airport, I felt enthusiastic about our reunion. As I approached the airport, though, my mood went through a dramatic shift. I didn't understand what was happening, but I began feeling less enthusiastic about seeing Maureen. Within seconds, it seemed, my evil twin had emerged. I was in a battle with myself. My evil twin began thinking of all the habitual complaints she has about Maureen, she began making an inventory of those complaints. The things I hate about Maureen began flooding my mind. (I'll spare you—and her—the ugly details, but *you* know exactly what I mean). Before I knew it, I was flooded with rage. It was simply amazing how quickly and completely the bad thoughts and feelings replaced the good. Although it felt like I had very little control in that moment, there was a compassionate voice trying to come through—however weak the signal was. It was saying, "What the heck is going on here? Your girlfriend is going to get off that plane excited to see you. She's been gone for days. Your complaints are history. She's done nothing to you in the last few days. How in the world could you be so angry at her?" The evil twin listened, knew the voice of compassion was reasonable, but she still couldn't stop the feelings. By now I was at the airport.

True to form, Maureen got off the plane in her usual openhearted, enthusiastic way and greeted me warmly and lovingly. I tried to greet her warmly and lovingly in return. I definitely did not pull it off. As we drove home, and as the evening progressed, the Great Wall came between us. She withdrew, feeling hurt and abandoned. I withdrew, feeling somewhat self-righteous, looking for some really great reason to blame her for the shift in my mood. I tried to explain my feelings to Maureen. That just made things worse. The more she distanced, the more I wanted to make all of it her fault. I went to bed as the Evil Twin. I woke up feeling confused, somewhat ashamed, remorseful, and contrite (emphasis here on *somewhat*). Although I tried to apologize and reconnect, I was still detached and angry.

Now, at this point, you may be wondering what this story has to do with the issue—how to keep your love alive. For me, that moment (and others like it), have everything to do with that question. For in that moment, I had a clear choice. I could dig in, as I did in the good old days, and make a case against my partner, assign blame to her, continue to judge and criticize her and justify my actions. After all, she is not perfect, and I could build a case for my feelings based on her imperfections. But the techniques I employed in the so-called good old days killed the passion, honesty, openness, and love in all my prior relationships. So the only choice I had now, in *this* moment, was to take a mirror, hold it to my angry, detached face and take full responsibility for my feelings and for my experience. Full responsibility. One hundred percent responsibility. Taking full responsibility means not reacting to that experience by blaming Maureen for my feelings, but by responding to that experience and seeing it as a part of the work I need to do in the relationship I have with *myself*—exploring, examining, inquiring into my response. As long as I hold Maureen responsible for my feelings, for my happiness and unhappiness, I give up responsibility for my own life.

So what exactly does taking responsibility mean? Well, for the next several days, I made myself look into the feelings that came up on the way to the airport. I *had* to look into these feelings because I could not, in good conscience, stay mad at Maureen. But I also did not want to make *myself* bad either. I tried to take responsibility while loving and being concerned for myself. In order to really *be* with my feelings, I had to make room for them inside of me. I had to cultivate a certain friendliness to them and to myself. It took a while to even have the willingness to look at them—and to look at them with loving-kindness. Once I did, however, they took me on a very interesting inner journey.

Here's some of what I learned. I remembered how difficult it is for Maureen and me to part and to reunite. My difficulties are very overt. When she leaves, I am highly anxious and afraid for her safety. Once she is gone, I am fine. When she returns, though, despite how eager my adult is to see her, my little girl is withdrawn. She is scared—who is this person? She is angry—how dare she abandon me! For years

I've compared this dynamic with the two-year-old children in the day care center I used to direct. They clung to their mommies in the morning as they were being left. "Mommy, don't leave me." They acted distant in the evening when their mommies returned. They ran away. They pouted. They were saying, in effect, "Think I'm going to act like I'm glad to see you after I've been abandoned? Fat chance, Mommy!" So one of the layers of my experience was familiar—my separation issues. However, those issues weren't sufficient to explain the intensity of my reaction on the way to the airport. I had to hold the mirror steady. Next I looked at the particular complaints that were coming up in the car. What could they tell me about myself? Most of my complaints had to do with my belief that Maureen wasn't taking good enough care of me. And while there could always be some truth in that belief, was that what was really going on? No. What was really going on was that I had been taking terrible care of *myself* lately. I had been avoiding some emotional processing. I wasn't taking good enough care of my body. I wanted, somehow, to make that Maureen's fault. I was angry because my personal needs weren't being met. But I was mad at her instead of me. That insight led quickly to another one. I saw that I was mad at Maureen because she knows how to take time off to go and play. She is a master at that. While my adult self admires her for this, my little girl is really jealous. She never learned to play as a kid and desperately wants to know how. Instead of figuring out how to play, she resents Maureen for knowing how. That was a very big and important piece of my reaction—which led to yet another discovery. This one seemed so obvious once it emerged. I was having a really good time by myself over the last few days, and I simply was not ready for Maureen to come home. I needed another day or two by myself. This processing of my experience took days, required help from others and represented very hard work. By the time I had gotten in touch with all these feelings, I had some understanding of, and compassion for, my evil twin. I could now sincerely reconnect to Maureen, and I could explain myself to her in a way that she could hear.

Keeping my love for Maureen alive, passionate, honest, and open requires deepening my relationship with myself. My love for her inspires me to see the difficulties that arise in our relationship as opportunities to become more self-aware and self-responsible. *And,* I expect the same of Maureen (who, by the way, wants the readers to know that she is perfectly willing to take 100 percent responsibility for her experience, but she's still trying to figure out what her experience actually is!).

I know that this kind of processing is only possible in relationships in which the partners have a deep-felt connection, a sense of safety, and an abiding love. I continue to be grateful that this is so in my relationship with Maureen.

In the meantime, don't ever forget, your love matters.

For one human being to love another: that is perhaps the most difficult of all our tasks, the last test and proof, the work for which all other work is but preparation.

Rainer Maria Rilke
quoted in *Challenge of the Heart:*
Love, Sex, and Intimacy in Changing Times
by John Welwood

Misery Side of Misery/Bliss Ratio

You shouldn't have moved in together. Living with someone has such a terrible misery/bliss ratio.

Noah, from the movie *Bar Girls*

This month's column is a musing on the misery side of the "misery/bliss ratio." It didn't start out that way. I had a couple of questions I was trying to respond to this month. The first reader asked me to describe "What is it like to live with a person for fifteen years?" The second asked me to elaborate on the list of "secrets to a successful relationship" published in my February column. The reader asked, "Could you make a couple of these items come alive?" Good questions, both of them, but my answers were sounding very uninspired. I had a partial draft written in response to the first question. I began that draft about three weeks ago after a blissful evening with Maureen; and the column was going very smoothly until I started writing about the not-so-blissful aspects of living together—the "misery" side of the ratio. The more I said about the misery of living together, the more my mood plummeted. Before I drowned in the misery, I decided to change topics. Of course, I was getting a big clue about HOW I WAS *REALLY* FEELING ABOUT MY RELATIONSHIP. But did I get it? No. That would have been too simple. I just chose to believe that I was stuck in the column and needed to shift topics. So I went on to Question #2 and went back and reread February's column. There I read the list of relationship secrets which, I had said, underlie the success of my relationship with Maureen. Awareness. Commitment. Compassion. Courage. Devotion. Gentleness. Hard work. Surrender. Truth. Willingness. Lots and lots of therapy. "Just pick a couple of these and make them come *alive*," the reader had asked. Simple request, I thought. I'll just whip up a quick response to that. But when I took a closer look at the list, I thought, "Who in the hell wrote that?" What do any of those words mean? They now seemed like a foreign language to me. There was no way I could elaborate on any of those concepts. No way I could bring them alive for someone else. They didn't feel alive for me. Second big clue about HOW I WAS REALLY FEELING ABOUT MY RELATIONSHIP. By now, I was starting to get the picture. I was feeling very discouraged about relationships. I was trying to write a column about love when I was feeling unloving and unloved. Who was I trying to kid? I was beginning to feel like a *Love Matters* imposter.

Well, one thing I can say about this column (especially when it feels like such a burden to write) is that it really makes me come clean about my own relationship. To myself. To Maureen. And, ultimately, to you the reader. The truth, once I dared to look at it, was that I was feeling pretty miserable about my relationship. I was kind of surprised, actually. I thought we were just coasting along, feeling maybe a bit disconnected, but nothing to worry about. When I looked deeper, though, I realized that when I was sinking into the misery description in the first draft of this column, I was lingering there too long. My relationship was feeling too much like Hell. When I saw myself unable to talk about those characteristics and qualities that underlie the success of my relationship, it was because I wasn't practicing anything from that list lately. The bottom line was that my relationship hasn't been feeling very successful in the last few weeks. Oh, no, I thought. What am I going to do about this damned column? How can I pretend to know anything about relationships if my own feels so distant and disconnected right now? How can I convey the importance of communication when I'm too mad and scared to talk to my partner? How can I promote gentleness and tenderness when I feel like killing Maureen? How can I explain openheartedness when my own heart feels like a rock? How can I preach truth when I've been practicing avoidance and denial? Well, needless to say, I realized I'd better put this column aside and go work on my relationship instead. I seemed to have gotten my priorities a little screwed up.

It turned out that Maureen was feeling similarly about the relationship. So we began "having it out," so to speak. I should tell you something about that, since none of the relationship books I read tell you what a real fight looks like—especially when the relationship has sunk into the misery phase. The fight began with the best intentions—using "I" sentences and all of that. Within minutes, we went from talking to yelling and crying (more crying than yelling) until there were wet tissues all over the house and two very spent-looking lesbians collapsed in bed. IT WAS UGLY. IT WAS SCARY. It was, also, exactly what the relationship needed. By the time the next morning rolled around, we had remembered how much we loved and liked each other; and we had freed the energy to begin working on all the things we had been sweeping under the rug for the last few weeks. The relationship now felt emotionally cleansed.

After our hearts had softened to one another again, we were able to see how and why our relationship had gotten so off track this month. I was grieving the deaths of two family members, had had bronchitis for a week, and was dealing with pain from a chronic back problem. Maureen was going through the anniversary of the death of her dad, had some other family issues in her face, and had also had her back go out. Our minds and hearts were outside of the relationship.

I wrote this column instead of trying to finish the other two so as not to be a *Love Matters* imposter. This month's column truly describes how miserable my relationship feels and looks *some* of the time. I think it reflects how most people's relationships feel and look some of the time. So many people think that, when their relationship feels miserable, they must be doing something wrong, that they are no longer in love, that the end must be in sight. And, for some people, that might be right. But what I've learned from living with Maureen for fifteen years is that our relationship is not some tidy little thing. Instead, our relationship can get to looking and feeling pretty messy at times. All that means to me and Maureen is that we are in a "dang" relationship.

In the meantime, don't ever forget, your love matters.

from **Body of Love**

V.
Will I still wonder
at hummingbird wings
that vibrate into shadows
when she has become as familiar to me
as the tree that draws her?

Will I feel
the vibration in my heart
when your fingers flutter
down my spine

my quickening joy when you
open the door after being away

when this life together
is what we expect?

I want to know

if the hummingbird
who hovers over my head each morning
during breakfast on the patio
will still be a miracle to me in ten years.

if your body warm with sleep
pressed close against my back after
the alarm has rung and been turned off

if the sound of your laugh
deep and full

if the shape of your jaw

the scent of your

the curve . . .

Judith McDaniel
from *The Arc of Love*
edited by Clare Coss

73

Bliss Side of Misery/Bliss Ratio

Relationships are truly a paradox. We spend half our time wondering whether we can possibly live *with* this person and the other half of our time wondering whether we can possibly live *without* this person. Last month's column was devoted to the former side of the paradox. This month's column is devoted to the latter.

A few weeks ago, while complaining to a friend about the difficulties of living with The Girlfriend, he challenged me to consider instead what it would feel like to live *without* her. In that moment, I had too much resistance to Maureen to take up his challenge. I needed to piss and moan a little bit more and romanticize about what it would be like to live alone. After our difficulties resolved, and Maureen and I felt reconnected, I began reflecting on my friend's challenge. Shifting the focus in the way he recommended was a humbling exercise. I quickly got in touch with what it is that I like and love about Maureen and why I continue to choose being with her. Indeed, when my heart is open, and I consider the possibility of losing Maureen, I can hardly bear the pain.

A few years ago at a workshop, I heard a very intriguing relationship concept from Stephen Levine. Stephen and his wife Ondrea have authored a number of books on death, dying, and healing, and they are two of my spiritual guides. Stephen recommended relating to our partners and all those we dearly love *as if they were already dead*. All relationships are impermanent, he teaches. If they don't end in divorce, they will someday end in death. Once we start relating to our loved ones as if they were already gone, our priorities will shift immediately. While I thought I understood this message cognitively, I had no experience within my body with which to relate to it. The idea clearly took hold somewhere in my consciousness, though. It was not too long before I began having some life experiences that helped me to integrate this teaching.

Two years ago, Maureen had a life-threatening illness. For a forty-eight-hour period, there was a possibility that she could die. I remember walking around our house panicked at the thought of losing her, praying for her recovery, mourning her absence. I found myself in Maureen's bedroom, a room that I always try to avoid. Maureen is a pack rat. Her room is filled with piles of her stuff—clothes, papers, books, a million and one mementos she cannot bear to part with. Her room (and these piles) have been an issue between us—a source of constant irritation and complaining by me and conflicts between us. That day, I sat down on the floor amidst all of her things, lovingly and tenderly holding them to me in an effort to feel close to her. In that moment, her piles took on an entirely different meaning. Were she to die, I thought, these piles might be all that I have left of her. Were she to die, I would probably enshrine that room and cherish her dang piles forever more. Now I began to understand what Stephen Levine was asking me to do.

A second life experience really helped to solidify the Levine teaching. Maureen flew to Minnesota last summer to visit her family. The trip came on the heels of another difficult few weeks we had spent together struggling with our usual relationship issues. Spring seems to be high season for our relationship struggles! I was mad at Maureen for not taking good enough care of me before she left. It went something like: "You haven't watered or mowed the lawn often enough." "Why don't you shop and cook more?" "You haven't won the lottery and taken me away from all of this!" And so on. You probably get the picture. A couple of days after she left, when my heart was already softening to her, an envelope arrived addressed to me in Maureen's handwriting. Inside the envelope was a copy of the $500,000 flight insurance policy she had purchased in the airport right before leaving. I was the named beneficiary. Maureen was trying to take care of me even as she was dashing to make her plane. Seeing the policy, and feeling her love for me, cracked my heart wide open. I burst into tears when I considered how my life would feel if Maureen had actually been killed in a plane crash and I had received the policy a couple of days after her death. Maureen dead. Me, a rich widow. I could then buy everything I thought I needed—a gardener to mow and water the lawn, a housekeeper to shop and cook. Would

I feel taken care of then? What an irony, I thought. Stephen Levine surely knows what he's talking about.

As often as possible, we need to change the way we think about our relationships and challenge ourselves to begin loving what it is we think we hate about our partners. It is so easy to get caught up in the problems and the pain and so hard to feel the gratitude and the joy. Changing the way we think about our partners and partnerships creates room to praise and celebrate them, as another one of my spiritual guides, Thomas Moore, recommends. Moore has written two books which inspire and comfort me: *Care of the Soul* (1992) and *Soul Mates* (1994). Moore calls marriage a "sacrament." "To care for its soul," he says, "we need to be priests and priestesses rather than technicians" (1994, pp. 58-59). Moore gives his readers a number of soulful ways in which to praise and celebrate relationships.

I took one of Moore's ideas and wrote Maureen a love letter this month. Moore feels that letter writing is a lost art, and I agree. While many of us write love letters in the early days of our relationships, we seem to lose practice along the way. Because I was feeling so open to Maureen and grateful for our love, I wanted to share my feeling with her. So I wrote her a letter reminding her and myself what it felt like to fall in love with her fifteen years ago this summer, what it is I love about her, what characteristics of hers I find so endearing and irresistible, why I honor and respect her, what I find so attractive about her, what it is about her love for me that is so compelling, what it is about our partnership that I cherish and adore. I really enjoyed writing this letter. It felt easy and joyous. Maureen was moved by it and very appreciative.

I've always valued Thomas Moore's concept of building a shrine to one's relationship. This month I have given a lot of thought to what life without Maureen would be like. It is a very painful thought. That kind of thinking really opens my heart to praising and celebrating my partner. At this time, I am in the process of building a shrine to my fifteen-year-old marriage to Maureen.

In the meantime, don't ever forget, your love matters.

Without warning
As a whirlwind swoops upon an oak,
Love shakes my heart.

Sappho
quoted in *Journey of the Heart:
Intimate Relationships and the Path of Love*
by John Welwood

Play

Question: You've let us know, through a number of columns, how intense your relationship with Maureen can get at times. So okay, do you guys ever have any fun?

Happy and Playful

Answer: Absolutely not. In fact, we have a firm policy against it. We're so addicted to the misery side of the misery/bliss ratio that we think fun in any form would end in divorce. (Oh, excuse me for just a minute. Maureen has something to say. What, dear? Oh, I made a mistake mentioning divorce. Divorce is not an option. Murder, maybe. Divorce, never.)

I think everyone who knows us would agree that Maureen and I have a pretty playful, lighthearted relationship. We have an incredible amount of fun and more than our share of laughter. In fact, if we could reduce the success of our relationship to one key factor, I think we both would say our sense of humor. Humor was a central ingredient in our initial attraction to each other. I think we are as chemically attracted to each other's humor as we are to each other sexually. It is a compelling attraction and one that has withstood the test of time. In fact, I think our relationship is even funnier now than it was in the beginning.

I happen to think Maureen is hilarious. Most people who know her would agree. She has a keen sense of humor and an infectious laugh. She is a gifted jokester with a great repertoire of jokes and perfect timing in telling them. She can also make a joke anywhere, anytime, about anything. In the bleakest moments, during a fight, in the midst of tears, Maureen will crack a joke, and we'll both burst out laughing. I've got a great audience in Maureen as well. She thinks I'm a riot, too. Although I have quite the reputation for a serious side, Maureen has inspired my humorous side. Behind closed doors, I can turn into a complete goofball. Although I can never remember an actual joke long enough to retell it (and if I could, my delivery would suck), I have a silly, witty, spontaneous side which Maureen really resonates to. I'll talk like a child. I'll play the fool. I'll tease and flirt. I'll play with words. I'll dress up like a dork. While Maureen's humor is often very directed and focused, mine is often unexpected and accidental. We kid, joke, rib, josh, and jest all the time. We just tickle each other's fancy.

We also make very good playmates. Maureen is, simply, my best time. It seems as if I am hers, as well. Our playtime might look uninspired to other couples, but it works very well for us. We don't share many hobbies, per se, have very few mutual projects or endeavors, and we really don't have that many shared recreational activities. We go to the movies, out to dinner, rent videos, make love, take vacations. We enjoy all of these pursuits immensely. But our all-time favorite thing to do (besides going to Paris, of course) is to just hang out and talk to each other. We are such good friends. We continue to find each other incredibly interesting. We are usually intrigued with how the other thinks, feels, and behaves (that is, when we're not being driven crazy by it). Usually, we can't wait to hear what the other has to say on any number of subjects. We are keenly interested in each other's lives, from the most mundane (how did your appointment go at the dentist?) to the most profound (do you really believe in reincarnation?). We share our dreams, our hopes, our fantasies, and our fears. We never cease to be excited and stimulated by each other. We just take delight in each other's company, so whatever we're doing together feels like fun. Sometimes, in the morning, we follow each other around the house while one is getting dressed and the other is drinking coffee, telling stories, exchanging gossip, complaining bitterly about the weather, planning how we'll spend our lottery winnings. Humor and play seem to be woven into the very tapestry of our relationship.

If someone were to ask how a relationship of fifteen years could still be so much fun, I'm not sure I could come up with an explanation. Did we learn how to have fun in a relationship manual? Did our therapy and workshops teach this to us? Did we watch our parents have fun and do everything they did? No way. None of the above. I think Maureen and I are simply blessed with a passionate connection that's been present since our first days together. There is definitely an electrical charge between us. It is because of our connection that we can laugh and play so hard; and the laughter and play help keep the connection alive. So, of course, the connection is kept alive by the intensely hard work that we do on the relationship every friggin' minute! While I have some ideas about how to nourish a connection when it is waning (or even when it seems to have disappeared), I have no ideas about how to invent a connection where it never existed. I believe it is critical for couples to have a healthy amount of chemistry between them when they first pair up. By chemistry, I mean a strong attraction for each other on a number of different levels. The connection will enable the intimacy. The intimacy will enable the play. Play is really a very intimate activity. You have to like the other person well enough and trust her enough to take risks, and you have to feel safe enough to be yourself in order to have fun.

So, yes, every once in a while, we put aside the fighting, the crying, the misery and have some good old-fashioned fun. How about you? By the way, do you know three reasons why chocolate is better than sex?

- You can GET chocolate.
- Good chocolate is easy to find.
- You can have chocolate in front of your mother.

In the meantime, don't ever forget, your love matters.

Laugh a little.
Laugh a little more.

Anonymous

Anniversary Story

This month I am going to share a story with you instead of responding to a question. On August 27, Maureen and I celebrated our fifteenth anniversary. I wanted to celebrate this occasion with the *New Phazes* readers. I think that all lesbians can appreciate how profound it is to stay together for fifteen years *and* to still feel grateful and blessed to have one another. I make the claim that fifteen lesbian relationship years equals forty-five heterosexual relationship years given the typical lesbian couples' lifespan! Our relationships are so fragile, so tender, so susceptible to breakups. To stay together for fifteen years and feel so in love with one another is truly a lesbian miracle and a cause for celebration. So in honor and in praise of this anniversary, I wrote and gave the following story to my beloved girlfriend. At first I felt too shy to share it with my readers. It seemed too personal and private. Plus, I wasn't sure it was of interest to anyone else. Maureen felt differently. "Lesbians need to shout their love from the rooftops! Besides," she continued, "Why shouldn't you publish this story about our beginnings. Your readers already know everything else about our lives!" So, the following is a story about our love affair. Perhaps it will inspire you to write the story of your love.

August 27, 1996

Once upon a time, in the summer of 1981 to be precise, two seemingly different women began noticing each other in new and interesting ways and decided to have lunch. Both women were deep in grief. One, Linda, was grieving the loss of what she believed to be the career of her lifetime. The other, Maureen, was grieving the loss of what she believed to be the relationship of her lifetime (which was clearly over but which she was still in). The tender hearts of these two women were burst wide open through this pain, and an opening was thereby created through which each could be truly seen by the other. One lunch was not nearly enough; and one lunch turned into many and was followed by dinners and many conversations that lasted into the night. They cried a river of tears together in that summer of 1981. They also laughed and played, rode horses, drank margaritas, and hung out with Linda's ten-year-old daughter Misty, who, the story goes, was already a good friend of Maureen's. At first the friendship between these women seemed a mere diversion; but then it became exciting and, pretty soon, it became absolutely erotic. By summer's end, these friends found it impossible to keep their hands off each other. Finally they kissed. Long and hard. Into the night. And there was no going back from there. Their passion was intoxicating. The more they touched, the more they touched, the more they touched. They had to say painful goodbyes to the other partners they loved because they had now become inseparable.

What an unlikely pair, everyone thought (including the two women themselves.) Maureen, from a large, fun-loving Irish Catholic family. Linda, from a smaller, serious, Jewish immigrant family. Maureen, a moviegoer, a nature lover, an athlete, a "look on the bright side" kind of gal. Linda, a bookworm, a lover of ideas, a politico, a "look on the dark side" kind of gal. Their personalities, their take on life, could not have been more different. Or so it seemed. But the overriding attraction happened to be their Souls. Their Souls were right at home with each other. Today, some fifteen years later, in the summer of 1996, this story finds them more together than ever.

Now these two women take delight in their likenesses. They laugh at the same jokes, covet the same beautiful things, take pleasure in the same food. They adore the same geography—Cannon Beach, Oregon—San Francisco, California—Paris, France. Blended together like warm milk and honey, they carry their pillows onto the same planes, cry at the same moments, share many of the same friends, buy the same greeting cards, smear wild yam cream on each other's tummies, light up when they see each other.

Ah, what did their Souls know that their little minds did not? Their Souls, indeed, held the greater intelligence. These two women, Linda and Maureen, were simply made for each other.

Magical. Mysterious. Miraculous.

The end . . . for now.

In the meantime, don't ever forget, your love matters.

The Heart Balloon

Despite the surrounding atmosphere
being the most "inhospitable on earth"
(the television documentary tells us) micro-organisms
never visible to the naked eye
live for millennia inside solid rock
encased in ice, there, in Antarctica.

Dormant, they wake each year
for five days only—Antarctican summer—
to find themselves enclosed alive.

Fragile, improbable, miraculous,
they propagate themselves in these
five days; they age, mature, fall back
to dormancy, and sleep until they die
within the sleep within the rock
within the ice within Antarctica.

And in that sleep who knows
what dreams may come of being
again alive?
For this? you ask, Why bother
to exist at all, for this?
What mindless desperate helpless drive
insists through them on living?

Despite the surrounding atmosphere,
a grey Thanksgiving morning one November
(the documentary of memory tells us), two women
waking in a bed of love astonished
see outside the window a crimson, perfect
heart mid-air above the city street,
fragile, miraculous, within
the granite air within rock-towered canyons
within the sleeping city.

One of the women whispers, We
must rescue it. She flings on sweater, jeans, boots,
to fly downstairs, out to the street, chasing
the heart balloon, chasing the wind it rides, dodging
the traffic, straining for its improbable perfection just
out of reach. A rebel shift of wind,
unlikely as five summer days preserved in ice,
breathes it within her arms.

The other woman, watching
from the window, cheers her on. Back
through the rock, back, back up the stairs, back
to their bed she bears it, lightly, in her hands.
For this? you ask, Why
bother to rise at all, the helium heart,
to hover against the ceiling's limits
leaking a love not visible to the naked eye
while two women stare at it in wonder?

Is the heart then a micro-organism
as well as a balloon of passing buoyancy,
improbably alive
in a surrounding atmosphere
the most inhospitable on earth?

For this? Only to be punctured, burst, and shredded,
frozen, thawed, refrozen, studded
by shards of ice until what breathes inside
the skin redensifies to liquid? To wither,
shrink, drift, deliquesce, descend
to dormancy, dream of having been alive?
To wake for five days only
and spangle itself mid-air, improbable?
You call the question up
through layered millennia of ice and rock:
For this? To let the mindless desperate helpless drive
insist through us on living?

This is Antarctica, nor are we out of it.

Rocks
(the documentary tells us)
preserve
within
themselves
our best,
our oldest,
and our ultimate
history.

Robin Morgan
Upstairs in the Garden:
Poems Selected and New, 1968-1988

Fair Fighting

Question: Would you please write about "fair fighting." I've always heard about it, but am not sure of the steps other than using "I" statements. Thank you,

A peacenik

Answer: "I" statements. Let me see if I understand what you mean. Like: "I hate your guts." "I think you're really stupid." "I never want to see you again."

Just kidding. . . . Well, sort of!

Is peacenik looking for some universal ground rules for fair fighting? Is she searching for some strategies for maintaining the peace? Does she want me to give her a formula for making emotionally correct "I" statements while fighting? If she needs any of the above, I'm afraid this column will sorely disappoint her. What I have to say about fighting defies all the conventional wisdom on the subject. By now, however, my readers have probably figured out that Maureen and I do not have a very conventional relationship. Or, at least, we don't think about our relationship in conventional ways. Maureen and I, over the last fifteen years, have developed a pretty forceful style of fighting. This style would probably horrify all the communication and relationship experts currently on the circuit preaching about "conscious conflict." I wonder, when I see these experts all lined up on the talk shows and I read their books, whether any of them has ever been in a REAL relationship. Maureen and I have made a conscious effort over the years to learn HOW TO FIGHT. We've learned that fighting is critical to the health and vitality of our relationship. And, believe it or not, there's been little or no discussion about how to fight FAIRLY. In fact, to me and Maureen the notion of fair fighting is truly an oxymoron. Fair is about the last thing we're thinking about when we are really fighting (as opposed to having a skirmish or an upset). When we're fighting, neither of us *wants* to be fair, nor do we think we *have* to be.

By now my readers are probably wondering what kind of a person, especially a so-called therapist, would ever think such thoughts, let alone say them publicly. I know I'm really going out on a limb here. But, believe me, this wasn't how I thought or talked either. Now, mind you, I never particularly *felt* like fighting fair in any relationship I've been in; but I believed the conventional wisdom about how adults were supposed to fight, how normal people were fighting in the privacy of their own homes. Good people. Sane people. Intelligent people. Such people fought fairly. They didn't raise their voices. They didn't say mean things. They didn't blame, make threats or judgments. When I measured my fighting instincts against what I believed to be normal behavior, I came up feeling Bad, Sick, Stupid, Guilty, Ashamed—great feelings for a healthy self-esteem! Much has changed during my relationship with Maureen. We have learned the value of a good old-fashioned fight. We now fight hard, fight more often, *and* feel good about ourselves and our relationship after our fights. We both credit a lot of this change to my relationship with my daughter Misty. It was really in that relationship that I learned how to fight, not fairly, but effectively.

When Maureen and I moved in together, Misty was a budding teenager. I was not at all prepared for her stormy adolescence. Misty had been a very sweet, even-tempered, and reasonable little girl. In fact, I worried that she was *too* compliant when she was in elementary school. I was shocked and scared by her teenage rebellion. Maureen had known Misty in her earlier, sweeter persona. She too, was unprepared for the level of conflict she would soon be witnessing. Misty and I fought about everything that parents and adolescents fight about—chores, dirty rooms, boyfriends, curfews. Our fights were loud, intense, unreasonable, irrational, knock-down drag-out fights. We screamed. We called each other names. We slammed doors. We made ridiculous threats. "I'm running away," she would say. "I'll pack your suitcase," I would respond. Since I was never allowed to fight like this with my parents, I somehow reasoned that this kind of fighting was good and necessary. Our fights generally never lasted very long nor, interestingly enough, did our angry feelings linger. Once we had exhausted our anger, the fight was behind us; and we returned to our more familiar way of being with one another—sometimes loving, sometimes indifferent. Whether our fights lasted a few minutes or a few hours, we always reconnected and felt fine about each other and ourselves.

In the meantime, Maureen, who was also a peacenik at the time, would be practically hiding under the bed if she were still to be found in the house. For Maureen, my fight with Misty was not over. She was scared to death. She had been a highly respectful teenager who went to heroic lengths to keep the peace in her family. She was afraid that the kinds of fights Misty and I had would leave permanent scars. What she observed in our household, however, challenged her thinking. Misty and I were, indeed, reconnected, and there really weren't any bruises. Maureen was fascinated with our outcome.

At this stage in our relationship, Maureen and I were not fighting. We were having what could be only described as minor and major "upsets." It wasn't that we weren't getting angry—it was that we were too afraid to voice our anger or acknowledge our differences. So, we would first try to hide any uncomfortable feelings we had. "What's wrong, honey?" she would ask. "Oh, nothing," I would lie. "Just had a hard day at the office." After a few days (or weeks) of lying, there would be a minor flare-up. One of my uncomfortable feelings would just slip out. I could see that it hurt Maureen, so I would spend hours backpedaling, apologizing for having said anything, lying some more. When the anger got big enough, we'd have a major "upset." I would directly express my anger, and Maureen would run as far as she could in the opposite direction, literally and figuratively. Or, she would start crying and retreat. I would immediately regret having said anything and start feeling like a really terrible person. While this dynamic was occasionally reversed, it was most often me trying to feebly express my feelings and her massively retreating. It would take days to get back on track. How we *got* back on track, only the Goddess knows. It certainly wasn't through processing the feelings. We just went on avoiding them. If we hadn't had such a strong connection and such intolerance for disconnection, we probably would have broken up after the first five fights. When we eventually reconnected, it took a long time, and the reconnection never seemed as complete as that which took place between Misty and me. In fact, I found fighting with Maureen to be hugely unsatisfying. Although it took Maureen longer to admit this, she eventually came to the same conclusion. We saw that our style of fighting was really unproductive, *and* we began noticing that our overall passion and good feelings for each other were waning. It was at that point that we consciously made a decision to learn how to have what we label as "real fights"—the kind Misty and I had had for so many years. First, however, we needed to articulate why my fights with Misty were so effective and what was getting in the way of Maureen and me having more effective fights. What did Misty and I have that Maureen and I didn't? And how could Maureen and I get it?

> These days, I thought, . . . I would have welcomed such a fight —true words hurled with a heavy hand. Hurtful yet still better than our present silent truce. Anger was the glue that held the marriage together.
>
> Shelby Hearon
> *Footprints*

What did Misty and I have that Maureen and I didn't? . . .

Of course, it seemed obvious once we started examining it. Misty and I had complete and utter trust in the bond that we had with each other and in the permanence of our relationship. We each knew that no matter how mad we got, what we said or how we said it, that neither of us was really going anywhere—for very long, that is. Our trust, love, devotion, attachment, loyalty were all woven into a "safety net" that contained our anger and kept our relationship intact. We could not stay angry very long. Our love compelled us to find a way to reconnect. We were familiar with each other's monsters and gave them permission to show up. We had loved each other long enough to trust that when we went away in anger and in hurt, we would always come back. We could remember the love. There would be apologies. There would be forgiveness. That KNOWING gave us the freedom to fully express our fury and our ferocity. We had a very solid foundation based on a strong early bond and many years of loving.

That degree of trust, that safety net, was not present in the early years of my relationship with Maureen. We have had to cultivate it. That degree of trust does not exist in the beginning of *any* relationship, and, sometimes, it never gets cultivated. That is why I must caution you about fighting in the way I am describing. It may not be for you. The trust has really grown in my relationship with Maureen and, along with it, the safety net has expanded to contain our anger. That safety net has given us permission to lose control and really let our anger out. I wish I could give you a blueprint for how to build such trust, because I believe fighting is an essential tool for maintaining intimacy. Clearly, Maureen and I, like Misty and I, had an intense early bond. What we had felt so good and so right that we were willing to really work on strengthening that bond. We just couldn't imagine ever wanting to be with anyone else as much as we wanted to be with each other.

How did Maureen and I go about strengthening that bond? How did we construct that safety net? While it's hard to articulate a formula for this (since all relationship work takes place on both conscious and unconscious levels), somewhere along the way we decided to make a COMMITMENT. It's been through this commitment, I believe, that trust has developed and the safety net woven. Now by commitment, I do not mean "til death do us part." We had both been down that road before, and we knew that mere promises did not guarantee the permanence of a relationship. The commitment we forged goes something like this: We commit to having the willingness to do whatever it takes to dissolve that which gets in the way of our connection. By whatever it takes, we mean *whatever it takes*. While we understand that sometimes our feelings are going to get so overwhelming that we feel like running away, or breaking up, or killing each other (so that we have to physically or emotionally go away for awhile), we have committed to coming back and working with the difficult feelings. Working with the difficult feelings means many things. It means talking. It means being honest. It means pushing ourselves to our uncomfortable limits. It means getting help. It means taking responsibility for our personal pain and all of our difficult feelings. Yes, taking responsibility for our feelings; understanding that our partner has not *caused* our feelings; she has simply *provoked* them. It means being committed to working with all parts of ourselves—our demons, our wounded little girls, our shadow selves. Understanding that our shadows will make us look and act crazy at times, but trusting that we will claim our own shadows and learn to live with each other's. It means allowing each other to be ferocious, even mean and blaming, *while* fighting, all the while knowing that *after* the fight, there will be a reckoning. It means knowing that we might be able to talk about our feelings *after* we've been angry; but while we are in the midst of our anger, we can barely talk. We must simply emote, blurting out our angry feelings in whatever way we can. We have come to understand that reptiles cannot speak in "I" statements.

As intense as my fights with Maureen have become, neither one of us has ever felt abused by the other. I find that rather fascinating, and I am trying to examine it. In part, I think it has to do with feeling so loved, so cared for, so respected when we are *not* fighting, that it provides a cushion for when we *are*. In part, it has to do with simply developing a tolerance for each other's fighting style. In part, it has to do with knowing that in every fight, each of us will be proven both right and wrong. In every fight, there will be some degree of truth and some degree of misperception. And, of course, it has to do with our commitment to work with these feelings *after* the fight. Explore them. Claim them. Tame them.

In prior love relationships, I thought the goal of fighting was to *win*. I needed to be right. I needed to make my partner responsible for my feelings. I needed to have my partner change or promise to change. What I have learned, in my relationships with both Misty and Maureen, is that the purpose of fighting is to get feelings out as directly, honestly, and fully as possible so as to reconnect. I have learned to trust, in my fights with Maureen, that we will reach a place where our feelings will be safe, honored, and accepted.

So, "peacenik," I'm not sure that I've answered your question in the way you hoped I might. Fighting is an area in which all couples must find their own ways. Fair is a very subjective concept. I can't define it for you. I'm about the business of finding a way of fighting that simply works. For me, that has become, "just do it," and deal with the fallout later.

P. S. I've really struggled with this column on fair fighting. I have written reams of material trying to find the right angle for a very tough subject. The perfectionist in me is still not satisfied. Suffice it to say that anger and its expression are broad, deep, and complex issues which this column will return to again and again. Although I use humor (and some sarcasm) in this column, I mean no offense to anyone, especially to any of you who have ever felt abused by someone else's anger. I know what abuse feels like and choose not to tolerate it in any form. If you feel you are in an abusive relationship (or any relationship in which the expression of anger feels intolerable), I hope you can find a way to get some help.

In the meantime, don't ever forget, your love matters.

Staying Together

Do you know why I think we stay together?

Because we fight in the car on the Beltway,
first about doing our clothes in a Rockville laundrymat,
then about everything: closeness, farness, love;
you mad enough to drive into an abutment,
me mad enough to open my door and jump;
both yelling, crying, past the Mormon Temple
lit like a Disney spaceship, which makes me
feel worse, like we're on the wrong planet.

After we both say, in different, loud frenzy:
How can anything be worth this? silence for twenty
minutes, the brief repeated glare of mile markers.
Then you ask in a mouselike voice if I would like
to go get in a hot tub with you, and I laugh.

Minnie Bruce Pratt
We Say We Love Each Other

Death of a Partner

Question: Eight months ago, Bella, my partner of six years, died of cancer. She had been diagnosed two years into our relationship and was only fifty-five when she died (my age now). Although our relationship had not been lifelong, it felt that way in its rightness. Neither of us had very long or very successful relationships before we found each other and expected and hoped that our relationship would last forever. I am having such a hard time with my grief and letting go of my loss. It is all-consuming. My family cannot understand why I am still so devastated even though they know Bella was my partner. My friends, although supportive initially, seem to be withdrawing now. My co-workers are starting to feel resentful that I am still so unproductive at work. Do you have any advice that might help me get past my pain?

Karen

Answer: I am so sorry to hear your story of loss and devastation. Four years battling cancer. Bella's death. Eight months alone. It is hard to even imagine the pain and terror of this experience. How exhausted you must be in this grief. While I know I don't have any words that would help you "get past this pain," Karen, I hope that my words might help to comfort you concerning your extraordinary loss. I believe we suffer lifelong pain with the death of any beloved person; and our task is to learn how to manage the pain, how to integrate the loss into our psyche and soul. Death of a beloved is not something we ever "get over."

One of the many painful aspects of grief is its loneliness. You sound very lonely, Karen. Your family, friends, and co-workers seem to be having a hard time with your sorrow, and this leaves you feeling as if something is wrong with you for continuing to be in so much pain. That makes me very sad for you—to have so much sorrow and so little support. It sounds to me as if those around you have had too little experience opening up to their own pain. They may be terrified by their own grief. If they are bringing expectations to your grief—judgment, withdrawal, resentment—these are merely reactions to their own closed hearts. Be patient with them—but do not let them define your sorrow, your partner's death. Define it for yourself. You are entitled to grieve as long as you need to. You might ask yourself, were it not for those around you, would *you* be comfortable to grieve as long and as deeply as you need to? Or, are your friends and family mirroring your discomfort with your own pain? If there are other things getting in the way of surrendering to your sorrow, what might *they* be? Other feelings—guilt, anger, fear, regret? What prior experience have you had with grief? How much permission have you ever given yourself to open to your pain? Although I've never walked in your particular shoes, I have suffered many losses in my life. The biggest barrier to my recovery was always my Judgmental Mind. It is the judgmental mind that says, "Enough now." "What's wrong with you?" "Pull yourself together." The best advice I've ever received regarding my losses has been to make room for them, to open to them, to surrender to them. Only then can we learn to live with life's sorrows. That is my expectation regarding loss. Let me learn to live with this pain. Believe me, were Maureen to die before me, I would never "get over it." Don't expect to get over or past your loss of Bella.

I'm wondering whether there aren't some ways to get support for your feelings. While loneliness will always be a part of grief, there may be more comfort available. I would highly recommend finding at least one person you can talk to who is comfortable enough with her own pain to really BE with you in yours. She might be an old friend, a new friend, a therapist, a grief counselor, a neighbor, a minister, a rabbi—anyone with an open heart and time to truly listen to your story. We have some excellent support services for the grieving in Colorado Springs—Hospice, First Presbyterian Grief Group, therapists trained in grief counseling. You might really benefit from hearing others tell their stories, having others to tell your story to, having your feelings validated and normalized, having someone to talk to in the middle of the night. Reaching out might still feel impossible to you; but if there comes a day when it seems easier, make a call. Find someone who cares.

When our beloved dies, we need to talk about her over and over and over again. Our friends and families do not necessarily let us do this with them. I think it is so important to find ways to keep your memories alive. One way is to write down the story of your relationship, the story of your love. Make tapes, albums of the cards and photographs you've saved. Ask for stories, photos, remembrances from Bella's family and friends. I recently attended a showing of an AIDS quilt made by the son of the deceased man. Not only had the father's friends contributed to the making of the quilt, but they sent letters and photos and told stories of the father's life. The dead man came alive for me although I had never met him. He became more alive for the son. Make a quilt for Bella. Build a shrine to her. Keep the relationship alive in your heart, Karen.

The most help I have received in the area of death and dying comes from reading and attending workshops by Stephen and Ondrea Levine. Two of my favorite books by Stephen are *Who Dies?* (1982) and *Healing into Life and Death* (1987). Their audio- and videotapes can be purchased through Sounds True Tapes and Warm Rock Tapes (see address at end of column). I also love the work of Elisabeth Kübler-Ross and highly recommend her books and tapes. I believe the loss of our homosexual partners is a uniquely devastating experience. Lonely. Misunderstood. Disrespected. Support by other lesbians and gays in similar circumstances might really be useful. There's a book that I like called *Write from the Heart: Lesbians Healing from Heartache*. It's an anthology edited by Anita Pace (1992, Baby Steps Press) and includes stories written by lesbians whose partners have died. It seems that some homophobic people expect us to heal sooner than our heterosexual counterparts. Maybe your family members are in this category.

Aside from thinking that you need to get past your pain, Karen, it sounds as if you are on the right track. Of course you are still having a difficult time. Of course your grief is all-consuming. Of course you are still devastated. You lost the love of your life. Trust yourself to maneuver this loss as best as you can.

*   *   *

Everything that has a beginning has an end. Indeed, the end is inherent in the beginning. Even at the moment of birth there is a contract with death. One in time will experience death of the other.

Stephen and Ondrea Levine
Embracing the Beloved:
Relationship As a Path of Awakening

In the meantime, don't ever forget, your love matters.

*   *   *

Warm Rock Tapes
P. O. Box 108
Shamisal, NM 87521

Sounds True Tapes
P. O. Box 8010
Boulder, CO 80306

To Beth On Her Forty-Second Birthday

I sat up all night and watched you sleep. I did,
all night. At midnight you became a year older
but you didn't know it. Swathed in my childhood
quilt, where so many of my childhood dreams
were born, most of which you have made come
true. Or perhaps you did know. It was just about
midnight when you hooked your toes in the
anklets of your socks and pitched them across
the room, as though preparing to run through
the dewy new grass. You have certainly been the
finest and most perfect part of my life. But I
sometimes wonder what you might have become
without me, without me hanging around your
neck in relentless poverty. Might you have become
a rich woman? Without my constant suckling
for approval and need for support, might you
have found a creative avenue of your own?

And so here I sit, watching you sleep, exhausted from the day to day taking care of me
instead of bursting exuberant into this new and
important year of your life. Just don't remember
me like this. Remember when I could haul fifty
pounds of firewood into the house single-handed
and lift you off the floor with one arm. No matter
what happens, we have something that most
people never do: the best. Happy Birthday.
I love you forever.

Jane Chambers
Warrior at Rest

Publication of *Love Matters*

A funny thing happened on the way to the typewriter. A book I didn't know I was writing got accepted for publication. On my desk, right now, is a letter from The Haworth Press of Binghamton, New York, addressed to me, Linda Sutton of Colorado Springs, saying in part:

> Enclosed, please find copies of the Author-Publisher Agreement signed with The Haworth Press, Inc., for the book tentatively titled, *Love Matters: Some Thoughts on Lesbian Love*. We look forward to receipt of the manuscript on or about March 31, 1998.

A collection of my *Love Matters* columns will be gathered into a book—sometime in 1999. Someone, pinch me quick. Could this really be happening to me?

It started innocently enough. I was reading my mail at the office, and waiting for a client to arrive, when I came across a catalog from The Haworth Press advertising books from their Gay and Lesbian Publishing Program. As I was leafing through the catalog I noticed something that piqued my interest: A request for manuscripts from "first-time writers." "Hmm," I thought, and filed it in my briefcase. That was sometime in spring 1996. At that time, I had been writing my *Love Matters* columns for more than a year. I had quite a collection. What my "hmm" was about was whether a collection of my columns might be worthy of a complete book. I sat on that thought for several weeks. One day I got bold and called the Managing Editor at Haworth. Surprisingly, I got right through. I told him about my *New Phazes* columns and my thought that perhaps they could be published as a book. He encouraged me to send in some examples of my work—even said he thought the name *Love Matters* was clever. Without editing or rewriting, I quickly submitted a sample of my columns to Haworth. It felt very daring, somewhat impulsive, and a bit foolhardy. Never for a minute did my conscious mind think anything would come of it. It truly felt like a lark. That was early July 1996. By the end of the month, I had a return letter saying my book proposal had:

> received a preliminary review in-house and has been for-warded to our program editor with expertise in this area, for further consideration.

Was I excited, or what? Had the whole process ended there, I would have been delighted enough. But lo and behold, by the end of August, I received a letter saying that my proposal for a book-length collection of my columns had, indeed, been accepted for publication by The Haworth Press.

> Congratulations on your interesting and informative work. We believe such a collection would make an exciting addition to The Haworth Press book program "Innovations in Feminist Studies." Thank you for thinking of The Haworth Press.

Thanking me for thinking of them! They said a contract would be in the mail and sure enough, it was. Between late summer and the end of 1996, I had the contract reviewed and signed, agreed to a manuscript completion date, and had begun working on a marketing plan with the publisher.

I am beyond excited and wanted to be the one to share this news with you. I can't think of anything else in my life (besides falling in love with Maureen) that has been so serendipitous, so fortuitous. That's part of what feels so sweet about it. I didn't have to *make it happen*. My excitement, of course, is tinged with terror. All my self-esteem issues are bubbling up. Are these columns worthy of a book? What if I publish it and no one buys it? Will I make a complete fool of myself? What will my mother say when she reads it? The stakes seem terribly high.

Yet there is no going back. This is an opportunity of a lifetime, and the excitement and the challenge outweigh the fear. Despite how unplanned and unexpected all this seems, I've decided to jump at this chance to write a book. All my life I've been enamored with books, with language, with words. While I've never thought of myself as a *writer,* it meets some very crucial needs—the need for creative expression, the need for daily routine and ritual. I have been an avid journal-keeper since adolescence. I love to write letters, essays, and speeches. I aspire to write poetry. I write at and with an IBM Selectric typewriter and find the pairing of the two—writing and typing—to be a wonderfully rich ritual. Only Maureen understands the love affair between me and my typewriter. I am in love with the sound, the feel, the touch, and the smell of an electric typewriter. It's sensual. It's exciting. To me, there is no thrill like turning on my IBM, listening to the hum, inserting a clean piece of paper, rolling it into place, putting my fingers on the keyboard, and beginning to type. Clickety-clack. The vibration, the rhythm, the beat of typing soothes and comforts me.

Writing comes easily to me when it is for my eyes only. I suffer over each and every word when it is for the public eye. *Love Matters* is both private and public. It is an experiment for me in style, content, and tone. It is intensely personal and extremely informal. It is vastly different from anything I have previously written. I have taken a personal risk in being so self-revealing, risking exposure and vulnerability for the column to be meaningful and authentic. The contract with Haworth has made this risk worth taking. So has the feedback from all my readers and friends. Hopefully this opportunity will challenge me to put words together more poetically, more powerfully. Perhaps, through this book, I can become a "real writer."

So that's the news for this month. *Love Matters* has made it into the Big Time. I want to thank *New Phazes* for accepting the initial idea for this column back in January 1995, and for continuing to print it and support it. Thanks, as well, to my readers for your continued support. Now, more than ever, I need your questions.

And last but not least, thanks to my lifelong partner, collaborator, and best friend, Ms. Maureen Stevens. I love you "truly, madly, and deeply."

In the meantime, don't ever forget, your love matters.

It's an act of faith to be a writer in a postliterate world. One disrobes one's typewriter with trembling and hope.

Rita Mae Brown
Starting from Scratch:
A Different Kind of Writer's Manual

Good Enough Relationship

Question: How can I tell if my relationship is worth working on or not? Or, do you think that any relationship can succeed if you just work at it hard enough?

Vicky

Answer: No way. I think that many relationships are doomed from the start and no matter how hard you work at them, they're going to fail. On the other hand, I also think that many more relationships could succeed if only we worked harder at them. The problem lies in knowing the difference. And that, of course, is easier said than done. Since we usually base decisions about relationships upon our feelings, and our feelings change from moment to moment, how are we expected to know whether this particular relationship is really worth the struggle?

To help discern the difference between those relationships worth working on and those that are not, we need some kind of measuring tool, a yardstick of sorts. Toward that end, I've been developing a concept about a "good enough relationship." This concept is a work in progress. I hesitate to call it a theory, a model, or even a tool because I resist theories, models, and tools as they apply to human relationships. They are too tidy, and you already know how untidy I believe relationships to be. The trouble with theories, models, and tools is that they lack soul—while relationships themselves are very soulful. Only through such things as poetry and song can the true essence of love be captured. Yet I also know that most people are really hungry for some way in which to answer such questions as the one our reader has posed. So I'll risk sharing my good enough relationship "concept" with you (along with my disclaimers about theories) and trust you to take from it what you will.

Actually the term "good enough" is not original. I borrowed it from Bruno Bettelheim's book on child rearing titled *A Good Enough Parent* (1987). I thought that was okay since he borrowed his term from D. W. Winnicott's theory on the "good enough mother." You've probably gotten the "good enough" drift by now. Bettelheim presents his premise in the introduction of his book when he states:

> Perfection is not within the grasp of ordinary human beings. Efforts to attain it typically interfere with that lenient response to the imperfections of others. . . . which alone make good human relations possible.
>
> But it is quite possible to be a good enough parent—*that is, a parent who raises his child well.* To achieve this, the mistakes we make in rearing our child . . . must be more than compensated for by the many instances in which we do right by our child. (p. ix)

I believe Bettelheim's theory holds true for many intimate relationships, be they mothering, parenting, or partnering. I've adopted and adapted this theory as a framework to use in my work with couples and especially in evaluating my own relationship with Maureen. I offer it to you, my readers, as simply one way of examining your own relationship.

Although I have given up the idea of having a perfect relationship with Maureen (and understand the damage to be done in even *trying* to achieve that), I can and do expect to have a relationship in which the mistakes, the imperfections, the problems are more than compensated for by the many instances in which the relationship feels right, happy, or satisfying. But what exactly does my relationship need in order to achieve such a "good enough" balance? Within my relationship with Maureen, I've identified three ingredients which, I believe, are essential to its success. While it's hard to imagine my relationship succeeding without all three of these ingredients in place, it is not essential to me that all of these be present all of the time. My standard is far more lenient than that. It is simply that they must be present *enough* of the time. So now, what exactly are they?

1. A Good Enough Partner
2. A Good Enough Connection
3. A Good Enough Commitment

Partner

The first essential ingredient in my good enough relationship concept is to have as a partner someone you feel is truly worthy of your love—at least enough of the time. Someone you adore. Someone you value highly as a human being. Someone you find virtually irreplaceable. Someone you feel proud to be with. Someone with personal qualities and characteristics that you admire and respect, find challenging and provocative. Something so special about her—the way she looks, feels, thinks, acts—that you can't help but think, "I want to be with *her.*"

I feel this way about Maureen—much of the time. She is quite precious to me. When I try to imagine life without her, it seems unimaginable. When I consider replacing her with someone else, I go blank. When I think about losing her, it feels absolutely unbearable. So much about her is worthy and valuable to me. She has a huge, tender heart. She is generous to a fault. She is patient, compassionate, exuberant, joyous. No one can make me laugh as much as Maureen. And, no one can make me cry as much as Maureen because she isn't *everything* I think I want or need in a partner. Her good qualities are not always present. She has qualities that infuriate me, hurt me, even terrify me. She lacks qualities I long for at times. Yet, on balance, who she isn't is more than compensated for by who she is. At the end of each day, it is still Maureen that I choose. She's simply good enough.

Connection

The second essential ingredient in my good enough relationship concept is to feel a deep and abiding love and connection for each other—and to feel this way enough of the time. By this, I mean a sense of closeness, connectedness, "in-loveness," a sense of safety that enables you to just "be"—to be/become all of who you really are, a sense of being seen, heard, felt, respected, and understood, a sense of passion—excitement, desire, enthusiasm—that is physical, emotional, intellectual, and spiritual.

I feel this way about my connection with Maureen—much of the time. I have no doubt about my love for Maureen or hers for me. Our connection feels deep, rich, and satisfying. Our hearts still soar at the sight of each other. We connect about politics, art, culture, psychology, spirituality. Yet there are enough differences to stay interested, to be intrigued, to provoke and challenge. We have fifteen and a half years of history to unite us, memories to nurture and sustain us, and there's also a sense of more to come—even a sense, sometimes, that the *best* is yet to come. Our connection feels like refuge, home base, safe haven.

Except, of course, when the connection feels like hell. Because a love this intense, a connection this passionate, gets to feeling very unsafe—even dangerous—at times. It gets confusing, confounding, and distorted. We distance, detach, disconnect, even run away occasionally. There are moments when the only connections we feel are hostility, rage, contempt. Or there are moments when the connection is weak—even nonexistent. As difficult as it is to admit such feelings, they are an important part of the good enough mix. This is what a deep connection yields—it yields highs and it yields lows. Yet, on balance, I can say that the lows are more than compensated for by the highs.

Commitment

The third essential ingredient in my good enough relationship concept is to have a commitment that makes you feel safe and secure—at least enough of the time. Commitment, to me, means the clearly articulated desire to have a permanent partnership and the willingness to work with whatever obstacles get in its way. Commitment means seeing relationship as a daily practice, seeing relationship difficulties as opportunities and challenges. Commitment means a devotion to personal work—yours, hers, and "ours." Commitment means having a vision of what kind of relationship you want and a process, a vehicle, a path to help you get there.

Maureen and I have a strong relationship commitment. It's been anchored by a ceremony and vows. It's not a "happily ever after" or "til death do us part" kind of commitment (although both of us dream about that). It's much more about seeing, understanding, and respecting the challenges and complexities that relationships present and being willing to commit to the extraordinary work that relationships require. Maureen and I have very little illusion left about love being easy. We view our relationship as a classroom—a place to study and come to better understand ourselves and the other, a place to challenge our perceptions of ourselves and our perceptions of each other, a place to learn how to take care of ourselves and how to care for the other, a place to challenge and dissolve the very duality of Self and Other. We are equally committed to seeing our relationship as a playground—a place to have fun, to laugh and joke, to play games, to flirt and tease, to be sensual and sexual, to be joyous and childlike. We are committed to being both reverent and irreverent.

Yet I'm not always proud of the partnership we've forged or the commitment we've made. Sometimes it feels hopelessly entangled, enmeshed, messy, yucky. There are times when I am ashamed of how unconsciously I/we have approached the commitment. There are times when one or the other feels completely unwilling to work on anything, to communicate, to open her heart. There are moments when we feel that this relationship is futile—that any and all relationships are futile. There are times when we want to walk out the door and never come back. And, all the while, we stay. Somehow the commitment we've made, at least so far, is strong enough to look beyond the day-to-day disappointments and see the whole of the relationship. Somehow we have developed a tolerance, a resiliency, an endurance that enables us to maneuver the challenging, difficult, and painful times. So, yet again, I can say that any disappointments regarding our commitment are more than compensated for by the many instances in which the commitment feels absolutely right.

This is what I mean about a good enough relationship. A good enough relationship doesn't feel good enough all of the time. For me, a good enough relationship simply needs to feel good enough—enough of the time. For now, that is at least part of the information I need to differentiate between a relationship worth working on and one that is not.

In closing, I have to say that the only thing more difficult than trying to have a good enough relationship is trying to write about one. Forgive me for any flaws, imperfections, or shortcomings within this column. I share it with you in the spirit of "good enough."

In the meantime, don't ever forget, your love matters.

It's hard to write about our relationship. I'm afraid of sounding smug when all I am is grateful.

Letty Cottin Pogrebin
Ms.

Jealousy

Question: *I love your column and have been gathering up the nerve to write this for some time now. I'm going to blur the details so my lover won't recognize our situation. I'm sure you understand.*

I have been dating a wonderful woman for over a year now. We have been taking it slowly because we both have been hurt in the past and want to be sure of each other's love. Our relationship has evolved to coupledom in that we see exclusively each other. We are definitely in love and plan to become wife and wife, hopefully, in the near future.

The problem is that her ex-lover of five years (who was unfaithful, which is why she's an ex) is still her roommate. They have been together for two years, but I am so threatened by this relationship that I can't stand to hear her name. It didn't bother me until I knew that I was deeply in love with my girlfriend. When I bring up the subject of "Don't you think it's time your ex moved out?" my lover gets defensive and says it's only a financial arrangement and I am being jealous over nothing. But I see that there's more there than meets the eye. There's a protectiveness that shouldn't be there. "She's having a rough time" or "She can't afford a place of her own." This woman makes more money than I do and, if I can do it on my wages, then why can't she? I'm not looking for anyone to take care of me. I'm an independent woman. So that's not where the jealousy comes from. I'm confused as to where it comes from. I feel like my girlfriend is being used and manipulated, but she's blind to it. To be honest, I feel cheated.

I have never felt like this before. I've never felt this much love for someone before. And I'm no spring chicken either!

So, Linda, what's going on? What can I do to make this situation better? Sign me,

Jealous?

Answer: Uh, oh. I've got some bad news for "Jealous?" (Whom I think I'll nickname J). YOU'RE IN A RELATIONSHIP! You're out of the honeymoon stage (where it doesn't matter how many exes your girlfriend is living with) and into the Reality Stage (where one ex girlfriend is one too many to tolerate). I'm afraid you're feeling a bit disappointed and disillusioned—"cheated" even—at the thought that someone else is getting the attention you now feel exclusively entitled to. I hate to be the one to tell you that how you're feeling right now is exactly how most relationships begin to feel when issues surface, whatever those issues happen to be—exes, sex, money, work, children, the in-laws—you name it. Relationships have a way of making us feel threatened, confused, cheated, angry, scared, dependent, etc., etc., etc. So, J, hang onto your hat. If you're signing up to be in a relationship, you're signing up to be vulnerable a lot of the time. Now I know that you would like to believe that it's just the situation with the ex that's making you feel so vulnerable. "The problem is her ex-lover . . ." You probably want me to side with you and tell your girlfriend that I, too, think it's time her ex moved out. Maybe you want me to say something like:

> Your girlfriend still lives with her ex? You must be kidding! And you're still putting up with this? You must be a saint! Tell your girlfriend to separate from her ex in thirty days or else—you're out of there.

Believe me, J, this column would be a lot easier to write if I could just stop there. But I'm afraid I can't simply side with you and have you think that if you just got the ex out of the picture, everything would be hunky-dory. 'Cause it just ain't so. Having said that, I don't want you to think I'm not sympathetic. I am very sympathetic, having had more experience with jealousy than I'd care to admit. And I haven't enjoyed one minute of it. Jealousy is about the most intense human emotion I've ever experienced. It's complex—made up of a number of different emotions—combined in a highly combustible way. It's confusing. You don't know whether you're having keen intuition or delusional paranoia. It's challenging. It takes you by surprise and throws you up against your deepest vulnerabilities. It's compelling. It makes you think and act in the most ignoble ways. So, believe me, I'm *very* sympathetic when it comes to jealousy. I don't want you to think for a minute that I don't think you have a point (or two or three), because I certainly do.

Here you are trying to have a new relationship, and your Beloved still lives with her ex. That's just a little too close for comfort, isn't it? Now I know the value that we, as lesbians, place on maintaining relationships with our former lovers. I'm very familiar with the arguments—extended family and all of that. But how close is too close? If one is still living with her ex, it would seem that *something* is going on beyond "she's having a rough time" or "she can't afford a place of her own." If this were a heterosexual couple, we'd have plenty to say on the subject, wouldn't we? I think it would be pretty dang impossible for you *not* to feel some degree of jealousy under the circumstances. I'd like to see your girlfriend re-evaluate the situation and figure out what's *really* keeping her from separating from her ex. Is she, in fact, still in love? Or is she still so unresolved about the ex's betrayal that she can't let go? Is she just not ready for a new relationship? Or what? These are questions only your girlfriend can answer. I think she needs to give you a bit of a break on the jealousy issue. Dismissing your feelings is probably not the most helpful approach.

But, I have to take the side of the girlfriend here, too. If I were in her shoes, I might be feeling pretty pissed right now. After all, she wasn't hiding the fact that she was still living with her ex when you began dating. How come you were willing to overlook that fact a year ago when you met? You may have appeared to be accepting of the situation back then, but now it's really troubling you. Maybe now you're starting to pressure, critique, and try to control the situation. Your girlfriend probably feels as if she's in a double bind. Perhaps she's over the ex but still cares a lot. She may feel that the very friendship is threatened. Maybe she's afraid that the jealousy she senses in you will creep into relationships with other friends. Maybe she feels there may be something deeper in your jealousy—prior loss and/or abandonment issues—which could be undermining or modifying your perceptions. Maybe she's getting scared about what she may have gotten herself into. Perhaps you need to give *her* a bit of a break on the ex issue and try to stop judging the situation in the most negative light. Could your girlfriend's defensiveness be justified?

Since none of us (you, your girlfriend, or I) know exactly what's going on, may I suggest that this problem may be an opportunity to learn a new approach to problem/issue resolution in the *beginning* of your relationship—*before* you develop a lot of bad relationship habits as a couple? My own experience suggests that, more often than not, it's how we handle the problem, rather than the problem itself, that can be lethal. I have three recommendations to make that, I hope, will help you start.

1. **Change course**. That is, change the way you are framing the problem. Set aside your need to be right and try to see the *truth* in your partner's position. John Welwood, in his book *Journey of the Heart: Intimate Relationships and the Path of Love* (1990), has a wonderful concept that seems applicable here. He calls it the "fourfold truth." Simply put, Welwood says that, in order to rise above our oppositional minds, we need to recognize "how truth and distortion are always operating on both sides of any relationship conflict" (pp. 124-125). If Welwood is right (and I believe that he is), that means that you and your girlfriend are both right—and you're both wrong. It means that each of you has some truth that you're trying to convey, some genuine need or feeling. But your truths get distorted in some way—through fear, projection, confusion, or denial. For instance, J, part of your truth *might* be something such as, "It feels too scary and threatening for you to be living with your ex." But your truth may be distorted—twisted into pressure and/or judgment—becoming, "Don't you think it's time she moved out?" If that's happening, that kind of distortion can come from many places—sibling rivalry, the loss of a parent, from your past broken heart. You're the only person who can identify where your distortion(s) come from. Your girlfriend might have a truth that sounds like, "Your jealousy is threatening to me—it makes me feel trapped." That truth might be distorted into a denial: "You have nothing to be jealous of." Her distortions may come from similar or different experiences—an excessively controlling parent, from deep feelings she's not able to name (let alone admit), or from real confusion over how to handle the situation. Again, your girlfriend is the only person who can figure out what emotional baggage may be influencing (distorting) her reactions and behavior now. It's human nature, as Welwood asserts, for each of you to see your own individual truths and your partner's distor-

tion. Please make an effort to take turns conveying your *genuine* feelings and needs while also sharing the ways in which your messages get distorted.

2. **Get some professional help with this issue**. Given the challenges and opportunities that this issue presents, I highly recommend that you seek some professional assistance. These are treacherous waters to be maneuvering by yourselves. It's very tempting to misdiagnose, mislabel, and misframe an issue such as this. It's very tricky. Given the newness of the relationship and the loving feelings you have for one another, this is the perfect time to learn the skills you need to work *with* problems like these. You can find help with a couple's therapist, a clergyperson, or by attending a workshop. The person from whom you seek guidance is less significant than *that* you seek guidance, so that this struggle doesn't wreak havoc with the wonderful aspects of your relationship.

3. **Buy *Permanent Partners: Building Gay & Lesbian Relationships That Last*, by Betty Berzon (1998) (if you don't already own it). Read, and then reread, Chapter 7 on jealousy. It's excellent. It's applicable. Do it immediately.

I know I'm sounding bossy here (and maybe cryptic, as well). It must be because this subject brings up way too many painful memories for me—my own feelings of jealousy, betrayal, loss, abandonment, rejection, and humiliation. It's *ugly*. When I've experienced jealousy in intimate relationships, I've gotten totally lost and bewildered. I didn't go for help when I should have. It would have saved me an enormous amount of grief. I hope that both of you value what you have enough to embrace the help you need.

In the meantime, don't ever forget, your love matters.

Jealousy

Nothing prepared me
for the way she smiled at you . . .

In a totally unfeministic fantasy
I want to rip her apart
piece
     by
        piece
be a diva drag queen like
Alexis Carrington and tell her
YOU HAVE TOTALLY OVERSTEPPED YOUR BOUNDS
as I withdraw my claws
recover my face and
pretend
you are a woman I loved
a long time ago.

Pamela Sneed
from *The Arc of Love*
edited by Clare Coss

Depression

Question: *When I met my partner, "Alice," eleven years ago, I was well aware of her history of chronic and severe depression. That didn't keep me from falling in love with her then, nor does it affect my love for her today. I didn't anticipate, however, how hard it would be to live with a depressed person. I hoped, foolishly perhaps, that my love could keep her spirits lifted. Over the last year, it seems her depression has worsened. She's withdrawn from me, feels worthless, is isolating herself from others and barely drags herself to work every morning. Alice is very negative about therapy or medication—both of which she tried without success before we met. She seems so stuck to me. While she has never had a suicide attempt (and she reassures me that she never would), she **does** make such statements as, "I can't go on like this." I am feeling scared, overwhelmed, and lonely. I also feel some anger and resentment building, and that makes me feel guilty and ashamed. I feel that I have no right to such feelings given how bad she feels and given my acceptance of her depression eleven years ago. Yet I am actually starting to feel depressed myself. Can you help me understand depression, and advise me on how (if) I can help Alice **and** myself? Or are these needs mutually exclusive?*

Mary

Answer: Mary, I am so saddened by your letter and the pain both of you are experiencing. I'm concerned that Alice is not getting any professional help. (Maureen, after reading this question, said if she could talk to Alice for just one minute, she would tell her to run—don't walk—to the nearest psychotherapy office.) And, I'm equally concerned that you are not getting professional help and are, only now, *starting* to feel angry, resentful, and somewhat depressed.

I got very depressed just reading this letter. I can't imagine how both of you have coped with this situation for so many years. It sounds as if there's a lot of love and a fair amount of resilience in this relationship. There's probably not much I can tell you—or Alice, for that matter—about the experience of depression. You have described it as well as a textbook might. Hopelessness. Helplessness. Lethargy/fatigue. Worthlessness. Negativity. Withdrawal/isolation. Suicidal thoughts and feelings. Depression can wear other faces as well—insomnia, hypersomnia, anxiety, restlessness, and hyperactivity among others. Although all of us will experience some degree of depression at different points in our lives, for others, like Alice, depression can become persistent, pervasive, and debilitating—affecting all aspects of one's being.

Some estimates indicate that there are 100 million depressed people worldwide. I've been told that one out of every ten American women is depressed. Medical doctors in this country claim that depression is one of the most common presenting problems in their offices. Depression is, in short, epidemic. Many factors can cause depression, either in isolation or combination: genetic predisposition; birth and childhood loss and trauma; stressful lifestyles—workaholism, substance abuse, poor nutrition, sedentary habits; medical conditions such as PMS, menopause, thyroid imbalance, chronic fatigue, hypoglycemia; side effects of medications; social isolation and alienation; spiritual voids. All these factors led one of my good friends to comment, "If you're not depressed, you're not paying attention." Yet when depression hits as hard and as long as it has for Alice, professional help of *some kind* is a must. While I'm sorry to hear that Alice's prior treatment was unsuccessful, that's insufficient reason not to try again. It's just not okay for the two of you to try to handle a problem of this magnitude by yourselves. It's not prudent nor is it safe. Depression can be fatal. It is estimated that between 25,000 and 75,000 Americans kill themselves each year. Depression is insidious. I believe it kills in ways other than suicide. My father suffered from depression that went undiagnosed and untreated for many years. When finally diagnosed, he required multiple psychiatric hospitalizations and powerful medications. A couple of years after his depression was diagnosed, he was found to have terminal cancer. He died not long after, and I was left wondering which condition actually killed him. Depression, once treated, can be enlightening. Depression left untreated can be dangerous. I believe that I inherited a predisposition to depression from my father. Thankfully, mine has been far less devastating than his, and I have had the benefit of more effective treatment. Nevertheless, I must be constantly aware of this tendency, and have a support team in place, or else my depression can get out of control. So I know, firsthand, the devastating effects that depression can have—on the depressed person, on her loved ones, and on their relationships. Alice's depression sounds as if it is out of control. By avoiding treatment, she risks a worsening of her condition, an alienated partner, and a deteriorating relationship.

In response to your question, Mary, "How can I help Alice and myself?" I believe you can make the biggest difference by insisting that Alice get professional help. Because Alice is so resistive to treatment and feels helpless and hopeless, you will need to become the bridge to that help. You might begin by letting Alice know the impact her depression is having on you and your relationship. You could talk about your fear, your anger, your loneliness, and your guilt. You need to understand that your feelings are normal and that Alice may benefit from hearing about them. You need to let Alice know that you are at the end of your rope and can't go on, yourself, without outside help. You could offer to do some preliminary research for Alice—some reading and some asking around about what kind of help is available. You might offer to take Alice to some appointments, if need be. But, if I were you, Mary, I would feel compelled to say that Alice needs to be in treatment for *both* your sakes. I believe such intervention to be appropriate within committed relationships. Maureen and I, as part of our vows, have promised each other that we will do everything within our power to take care of ourselves (our minds, hearts, bodies, and spirits), and we give each other permission to step in if we feel that vow is being broken. I believe that you are entitled to take some action given the seriousness of Alice's depression.

To help convince Alice, you need to know that there are far more treatment options available for depression than ever before (and certainly more than there were eleven years ago). Whether one sees depression as a psychological illness or as a spiritual awakening, as a symptom or as a teacher, as a curse or as a blessing (or all of the above), there is some kind of help available. There's Prozac or St. John's wort. There's psychotherapy or meditation. There's dream analysis or body work. There's EMDR (eye movement desensitization and reprocessing procedure) or yoga—or all of the above. There *is* something out there that might actually relieve Alice's depression. If I were Alice, I would begin by having a complete physical examination by a qualified practitioner experienced with depression—whether allopathic or naturopathic. Believe it or not, this step is often overlooked, and underlying medical conditions are not discovered. Once this step is taken, and depending on what is found, the next step might be to seek the right kind of therapy (or combination of therapies) for the depression.

Mary, you were far from foolish in thinking that your love might keep Alice's "spirits lifted." There is much research documenting the healing power of love. Indeed, a loving relationship can help one to overcome depression. For instance, in a recent article on depression by Karen Ocamb in the spring 1997 issue of *Treatment Today,* Mike Wallace credits his wife, Mary's, "dedication and support" to his being able to seek treatment and overcome his depression. William Styron (1990) describes his wife, Rose, in his must-read book, *Darkness Visible,* as the "endlessly patient soul who had become nanny, mommy, comforter, priestess and, most important, confidante . . . " (p. 57). Loving spouses alone, however, could not cure their disorders. Alice needs a support team with you, Mary, as one of its members. You need your own support team. As you are too well aware by now, depression can be contagious. You have needs that are as important as Alice's. I can only guess what they might be—talking with friends and family, having your own therapist, going to a support group, spending time away from Alice, taking a vacation. Whatever your needs are, I strongly urge you to place a high value on them. If your mood continues to deteriorate, you'll be of no help to Alice. You have been a patient, loyal, and loving partner to her. Now it's time to get some help.

Thanks so much for this question. I suspect that there are many others out there, like you and Alice, suffering in silence. I'm closing this column with a short reading list on depression.

In the meantime, don't ever forget, your love matters.

*   *   *

- *When Someone You Love Is Depressed: How to Help Your Loved One Without Losing Yourself,* Laura Epstein Rosen and Xavier Francisco Amador
- *Darkness Visible: A Memoir of Madness,* William Styron
- *Natural Alternatives to Prozac,* Michael T. Murray
- *Overcoming Depression: The Definitive Resource for Patients and Families Who Live with Depression and Manic-Depression,* Third Edition, Demitri and Janice Papolos

I measure every Grief I meet
With narrow, probing, Eyes
I wonder if it weighs like Mine
Or has an Easier size.

Emily Dickinson
Poems, Third Series (1896)
from *The Beacon Book of Quotations
by Women* by Rosalie Maggio

Solitude

Question: Although my lover, Barb, and I have been together for over five years, we continue to go round and round on the subject of solitude. My solitude, that is. I guess I've pretty much been a loner most of my life, and living with someone has really been a challenge. For the most part, I love it and have adapted; but in order to not feel too crowded, I find I need a fair amount of time alone. Barb feels threatened by my solitude. In the beginning, she was distrusting of it, but now it is not distrust so much as it is her own loneliness, at least that's what she's saying now. Barb feels kind of scared and empty when I am gone, yet she knows that's not a good enough reason to tell me not to leave. Could you give us some advice for this problem?

Shelley

Answer:

. . . a good marriage is one in which each appoints the other guardian of his solitude. . . . All companionship can consist only in the strengthening of two neighboring solitudes, . . . for when two people both give themselves up in order to come closer to each other, there is no longer any ground beneath them and their being together is a continual falling.

Rainer Maria Rilke
quoted in *Challenge of the Heart:
Love, Sex, and Intimacy in Changing Times*
by John Welwood

Rilke's wisdom pretty much sums up my sentiment here. My best advice to Barb would be for her to learn how to stay connected to herself, *and* Shelley, when they are apart. Without solitude, it seems to me, there *can be no* togetherness. I've probably made an adequate case in prior columns for how messy and impossibly difficult all relationships are—what with our grief issues, our power and control issues, our attachment and separation issues (just to name a few). The *least* we can do to make our relationships work a little better is *to take a break from them*, as often as we can. I have come to a place in my life where solitude has become my ally. At one time I would have called it my enemy. Life with Maureen is what changed all of that.

Maureen takes off several times a year on various trips. In fact, she's gone right now on a two-week trip to Minnesota to visit her family (no kidding, *two weeks* with the family!). Maureen has taken off like this ever since we've been together—two weeks in the summer, a week at Christmas, weekends here and there. Even when she's at home, she's off spending time with her family, or golfing, playing tennis, going to the movies. She's an independent cuss! In theory, I love that about her. In practice, I've sometimes had a very bad time with it. In our earlier years, I resented her time away, even when I was invited! Given how paradoxical those feelings were, I had a tough time trying to justify them. That didn't keep me from trying, however. I would argue that we didn't spend enough time alone. But that was a lie, and I knew it. I would argue that we didn't take enough vacations *together* alone. But that was a lie, and I knew it. I would argue that she liked her family and friends better than she liked me. And, of course, that, too, was a lie, and I knew it. *What was true* was that we had a pretty balanced relationship—with time together *and* time apart—but some of the time that I spent by myself, my very young and tender feelings would surface and leave me so vulnerable that I would go to any extreme not to be alone with them. One of these "extremes" was resenting Maureen for abandoning me. I had a repertoire of other extremes—workaholism, chronic busyness, obsessive community activism. Somewhere along the way, these extremes became more uncomfortable and dysfunctional than the vulnerable feelings they were designed to protect; so I decided to confront the feelings instead. I sought out a number of resources to help me do just that. One of the resources was a book titled *An Unknown Woman: A Journey to Self-Discovery* by Alice Koller (1981). It is a true story written in novel-like form about Alice's journey to find her true self. At thirty-seven, she goes off to Nantucket in the dead of winter to look for and, hopefully, heal the source of her despair. What she discovers about her despair, in her solitude, is that she has spent her entire life reflecting herself through the eyes of others—parents, lovers, employers, friends. In their absence, she has no authentic sense of herself. She lives in virtual seclusion for several months and, in an agonizing, painstaking way, learns to connect to her own feelings (her needs, wants, thoughts) until she begins hearing *her own voice*. It's a powerful story and a wonderful blueprint for self-intimacy. It inspired and challenged me to cultivate the practice of solitude as a way of deepening and strengthening my relationship with myself.

Shortly after reading Koller's book, I took my first solo vacation. I had traveled many times by myself, but always with a specific focus—workshops, visits with family, business trips. I *never* considered a vacation alone. That vacation, and others that I have taken since, was extremely enlightening. Connecting to my wants and needs was not nearly as difficult as I had expected. Nor was I as frightened as I had imagined. What really blew me out of the water was seeing how different my needs and wants looked when no one else was around. I was feeling and acting in ways that were completely unfamiliar. I discovered aspects of self I never knew were there. I felt unbelievably *unencumbered*. Everything felt expansive—time, energy, thoughts, feelings. It was mind-boggling and continues to be. Now, it's not that Maureen is so controlling or that anyone or anything in my life actually holds me back. The difference is completely internal. *I hold myself back* around others. I *encumber* myself. I project, distort, defend, transfer, assign, however you choose to frame it—I lose myself around others. I give myself up. Solitude has shown me the extent to which I do that, and solitude is teaching me the way back to myself.

Solitude is not always a friendly place. Alice Koller knows that and so does Barb. That's why she wants to avoid it. Our worst demons can emerge when we're alone—such as the fear and emptiness that surface for Barb. My demons have really been appearing in the week since Maureen left, causing her to ask on the phone, "Why do you think you take such a dive when I leave? You seem so happy to have me gone." The answer seemed very easy. "Because *you are gone*," I said. Sure, there are many parts of me that really need a break from the relationship and welcome her departure. But when she's around, her mere presence can serve as a safety net for my deepest, most painful feelings. That safety net can work in a number of ways. I can defend against those feelings by somehow making them her fault. Or, I can defend against them by seeking her comfort too soon, thereby "breaking my fall." In either case, I might not go deep enough into my feelings to find out what the *real* problem is.

Let me show you how this works. So, there's no Maureen around this week, and I'm just trying to live my life—enjoying an empty house, total control of my space, lots of free time, nobody around to bug me—when THE DEMONS come knocking at the door. Of course, they arrive when I'm trying to write this damn column. I had been trying for days to say something halfway intelligent, but it was eluding me completely. One morning I sat down at the typewriter raring to go. I had the time. I had the energy. I had the idea. WRONG. VERY WRONG. One paragraph into the column, my correcting tape ran out. It took me over half an hour to get the new one installed—despite the fact that I've changed ribbons for fifteen years. That was the only trigger I needed to begin THE DESCENT. Before I knew it, THE CRITIC was in full swing. "How could you be so stupid! What's wrong with you? How will you ever learn to use a computer! You can't write! Who do you think you're trying to fool! You really are a WORM!" Etcetera. Etcetera. Etcetera. My feelings of inadequacy were totally in my face. Now, were Maureen here, I might defend against these feelings by trying to make *her* out to be THE WORM. Or, short of that strategy, I might just tell her about the "I am a worm" feelings as they were surfacing. Loving me as she does, she would try to protect me from these feelings by telling me all the reasons why I wasn't a worm.

That comfort might serve as a Band Aid, another kind of defense against the inadequate feelings. With Maureen gone, there was no defending against these feelings. I really had to work through them at a deeper level. Now, if I'd tried hard enough, I'm sure I could have found some way to distract myself. But I can tell you, if you spend enough time alone, your deepest feelings are going to be in your face. And mine really *need* to be if I'm ever going to make friends with my demons. This week I did—at least for now. After hours of self-loathing and self-deprecating, there was a shift, and I eventually got to the *real source* of my pain. For me, the low self-esteem is simply a "false" bottom. There are always more primary and more interesting feelings underneath. Mine are about whether or not I have a right to exist in the world, about feeling wanted at a very deep level, about being loved for who I am, not for what I do. These are some of my core issues and they underlie many of my dynamics. When Maureen (or anyone else) is around, I can easily be sidetracked from this core emotional work. Solitude, for me, facilitates such work.

Solitude now sustains and nurtures me, renews and restores me, *and* challenges me to my deepest core. It enables me to be in relationship with self *and* it enables me to be in relationship with Maureen. That's why I began this column with Rilke's words. I have a feeling that Barb and Shelley knew what I was going to say before I said it. I hope my experience can guide and support their own work.

In the meantime, don't ever forget, your love matters.

July Morning

once again the cactus
is filled with mercy
offered in blooms of soft light

        it knows no shame
        for its life of thorny protectiveness

    as I am NOW
    hold me

white and lavender trumpets of lilac
have retreated to their meditative state

        they do not harbor feelings of isolation
        in their graceful solitude

    as I am NOW
    Sanctify me

the showy forsythia has conjured up
a staggering growth of greenery

        there is no judgement surrounding
        its search for revelation of self

    as I am NOW
    nurture me

cycles in the wonder of becoming

        no sarcasm is voiced concerning
        their disappearance and reemergence
        boundaries are not placed
        on their need for ritual

    as I am NOW
    honor me

                        Patti Grimes

Mothering

Question: I am a lesbian in my late thirties in a long-term, stable relationship. As long as I can remember, I have wanted children. I teach elementary school, love kids, and feel very comfortable with them. My partner, Kathryn, very much desires children, as well. When I first came out as a lesbian, I thought having children would be out of the question. I grew up in an alcoholic family and felt so much shame about my father's condition, the family secrets and lies. I never felt comfortable bringing any friends to my house. I don't want to bring a child into the world and make her life difficult because of my differences, even though I know my differences are not the same as my dad's. I look around now and see so many lesbians and gays having children, and I wonder about myself. I know that you have a grown child and I wonder how you made the decision to have a child, and what that's been like for you and for her. When did you tell her? How has she accepted it? How has it affected your relationship with each other? How open has she been about it and how has it affected her relationships with others? What advice would you give two lesbians who are considering having children?

Natalie

Answer: First, I need to say that when I made the decision to have a child, I was a twenty-five-year-old, happily married heterosexual. I had absolutely no *conscious* idea about the course my life would soon take—that I would become a radical feminist, divorce within six years, fall in love with and want to be with women. So, the decision facing Natalie and Kathryn is *very* different from the one I made. And, the childhood experiences my daughter Misty has had—the devastation of divorce, life in two homes, two full-time working parents—may not be at all comparable to the kind of life Natalie and Kathryn might provide to their child/children.

I can say that raising Misty has been, and continues to be, my most significant life work. No other relationship or experience that I have had has had as much meaning, importance, or impact. Would I have *consciously* chosen to have a child as a lesbian mother? Probably, but I can't possibly say for sure. All I can say now is that life without Misty is simply *unimaginable*, and I would never want to deny another human being the opportunity of parenting because she happens to be a lesbian. I would only hope that *anyone* choosing to raise children, *however* they came into the family, would have a heart sufficiently open to be able to embrace the joys *and* the sorrows of parenting. While it would be foolish to deny the impact my lesbianism has had on Misty's life, nothing has had more impact than my *capacity to love*. Through loving Misty well, I believe I have helped prepare her for the many challenges that life presents—including my own sexuality.

Loving Misty well has not come naturally. Although Misty was a planned for (and very much wanted) child, I can look back now and see how totally unprepared I was for the job of mothering. Oh, on the surface, I looked good enough—had the right "resumé," a seemingly happy marriage, good education, enough money, strong support system, and a keen interest in children; yet underneath, I was a scared, needy little girl myself. Like my illusions about the nature of all other intimate relationships, I expected mothering to be a lot easier. I really had to grow into the job over many, many years. Of course I made countless mistakes and, I hope, had many successes as well. I had a burning *desire* to be a good mom and enough humility to get the help that I needed to be able to achieve that desire. Becoming a lesbian was just one more hurdle to jump as a mother.

Misty was about six when I began dating women while still dating men. I told Misty about my emerging lifestyle as it was happening, although she was really too young to understand. There were other, more confusing, events in Misty's life during this time. She was trying to cope with her parents' divorce, the loss of her family as she knew it, joint custody, and day care. My sexuality was the least of her problems. She was overwhelmed by loss and change. I'm sure that she desperately wanted some stability, security—some sense of "normalcy." *Nothing* was normal anymore. My relationship with women during her elementary school years may not have been her favorite thing (although she had excellent relationships with my women lovers), but it clearly wasn't the biggest focus in her life. My sexuality became more of an issue during her adolescence and young adulthood as her own sexuality was emerging. At that point in her life, as for all teenagers, what her peers thought of her meant everything. Developmentally, her task was to separate from me and become her own person. Concurrently my choice to be with women became more firmly rooted.

I had to learn how to handle issues of my lesbianism as they surfaced—again, through trial and error. Misty was teased and taunted about my lesbianism in elementary school. She felt embarrassed and ashamed. She went through a stage, in junior and senior high, when she didn't want me to have my lovers around if her friends were sleeping over. She even tried blackmailing me once when she was still in elementary school. I was trying to get her to go to bed, and she screamed, "If you don't let me stay up later, I'm going to school tomorrow and tell everyone on the playground that YOU ARE A LESBIAN!" So, some of our stories are painful and others are pretty comical. The older Misty got, the more comfortable she became with my lifestyle. I noticed a correlation between my own acceptance of my lesbianism and her acceptance of my lesbianism. I tried to be very sensitive to the impact my lifestyle was having on her and to respond to her with love, compassion, thoughtfulness, and respect for her needs. Whatever discomfort—anger, embarrassment, sadness—she had related to my sexual preference, it did not undermine our relationship. Our love for each other transcended that. Once Misty became more mature, and had a strong enough sense of herself, she became more and more accepting.

In fact, were it not for the discrimination our children face *because* of the judgments and prejudices against homosexuality in our culture, they would most likely be indistinguishable from children reared in any other family constellation. Misty had no difficulty with my sexuality when she was very young—*before* she knew that other people had a problem with it. Within our own family (her dad, our extended family, our friends) my lesbianism was, thankfully, accepted and supported. In other words, it was not until she ventured *beyond* that protected circle that she encountered discrimination. *That* discrimination and the threat of further discrimination, *not my sexuality*, were what wounded her. Ironically, as with racism—or any other ism—it's the people who rail against children being brought into "such damaging situations" who do the damage they supposedly want to protect children *from*. Consequently, an additional responsibility taken on by homosexual parents is the commitment to give our children the coping skills and resources they need to deal with such a crazy world.

Parenting is the most difficult job on earth—and the most rewarding—for those who take it on. Misty has gained a great deal *because* she is the daughter of a lesbian. She has acquired a great sense of fairness and justice. She is wonderfully tolerant of differences and has affection for minorities of all kinds. She has a tremendously open heart, lots of personal courage, and a very expansive view of love. Putting aside my motherly prejudice, I think Misty is an exceptional woman. It's incredibly satisfying to know that Misty admires and values my relationship with Maureen and sees us as a rare example of a truly loving partnership. She is open with her friends, and she respects my commitment to be "out" in the community. This chapter in our lives has a happy ending. Natalie and Kathryn, I wish the same for you.

I've asked Misty to share some of *her* thoughts about being the daughter of a lesbian. Since Misty was born into a heterosexual family, her experiences may be different from those of a child born into a "two-mom" family. Nevertheless, I think they address some of Natalie's concerns.

Misty's Response:

On August 27, 1991, I experienced a momentous shift in the way in which I viewed my mother's lesbianism. Although I had been aware of her sexual preference for years, it was on that date that I unconditionally accepted her lifestyle and, at the same time, came to understand how fortunate I was to have her relationship with Maureen as a model. To me, love is comprised of several elements— commitment allows for safety, respect keeps the connection mutual, passion creates a new and exciting day every day. Also, learning to love ourselves offers a gift to our partners which is of far greater value than any material object. My mother's relationship with Maureen represents this definition of love. August 27, 1991, my mother's and Maureen's tenth anniversary, marks the day that I was able to recognize and celebrate their love.

Kierkegaard reminds us that, "Life can only be understood backwards; but it must be lived forwards." It took many years for me to come to an unconditional acceptance of Mom's sexuality. Although my memory is somewhat foggy, I think my mom told me that she was a lesbian when I was about six years old. Without a clear understanding of sexuality in general, I don't think I had much of a grasp of the implications of having a lesbian mother. However, I do recall thinking that *whatever* a lesbian is, it's different and, to me, different was cool. When I proudly announced to my friends that my mother was a lesbian, I was unprepared for their responses. I was teased, excluded, and laughed at. At that point, of course, I began to resent my mom for being different. I felt that her choices made me different as well. It's unrealistic to expect a young child to be able to separate her identity from that of her parents and, from that point forward, I was ashamed of who my mom was and certainly avoided discussing it with friends. It was difficult to simultaneously admire and resent my mother.

Fortunately, my mom was aware of my resentment and of society's ignorance, and she took responsibility for helping me deal with the challenges that her lesbianism presented to me. Communication was the key to confronting the challenges and, although there were times that our communication wasn't ideal, the lines were always kept open.

In retrospect, I can see that the greatest difficulty for me (as for almost every adolescent) was in separating from my mother and discovering my own identity. As a teen (and even into early adulthood), I chose not to tell most of my friends about my mother's lesbianism. I was afraid that they would assume that I was gay. Keeping that big secret definitely inhibited my ability to establish solid connections with others, know and accept myself, and develop my own identity. I changed friends often, and I made poor choices along the way.

Obviously, many teenagers face these kinds of problems—regardless of their parents' sexual preference; but I purposely address this issue to emphasize my view that it's critically important for all parents to facilitate their children's recognition and sense of Self. I am in the process—maybe a lifelong process—of becoming aware of who I am and what I want to be. Therapy has helped and, in some way I can't quite explain, I now understand that I had to separate from my mother before I could unconditionally accept her lesbianism.

I admire, respect, and appreciate my mom for everything she is. I love her for having the courage to be true to herself—even when that wasn't easy. I hope that I will continue my own self-exploration with the courage and persistence my mom has modeled for me.

In the meantime, don't ever forget, your love matters.

But what mother and daughter understand each other, or even have the sympathy for each other's lack of understanding?

Maya Angelou
from *The Beacon Book of Quotations by Women* by Rosalie Maggio

Singlehood

Question: I seldom read your column because I'm chronically single and reading about relationships feels either irrelevant or like salt upon a wound. Someone once said to me that being a single lesbian is worse than being a single straight in this town. I can testify to the fact that it is, indeed, loneliness compounded. While being single almost anywhere isn't easy, most coupled lesbians are not only insensitive to their single lesbian sisters—but often downright cruel. Singles are ignored socially and/or treated with suspicion. While the world would like most lesbians to be invisible, single lesbians are made invisible by other lesbians.

While I recognize your bread and butter is couples and relationships, maybe just once in the umpteen times you've written your column, you could give loneliness, alienation, singleness in the Colorado Springs lesbian community a few lines. Thank you,

Francine

Answer: A good friend of mine, upon hearing my dilemma—that of a chronically married person trying to respond to a chronically single one—volunteered to guest-write this month's column. As a lesbian with considerable experience in being single, she, far more than I, has the credentials called for to answer Francine's question, and I thank her.

Linda

Dear Francine,

Having recently been single for a period of twelve years, I can relate to wanting to read about the single experience. Well . . . , now I'll try to write the article I always wanted to read. And, while my singlehood may not resemble your singlehood, Francine, at least it won't be about coupledom. A book title? *Life As a Single Lesbian,* or, *How Do You Prove You're a Lesbian if You Have No Girlfriend?*

My first few years of being single were the worst. I struggled with loneliness, self-doubt, and anger at other people's assumptions. The loneliness would hit me on weekends. I'd be busy working all week, and come Friday night, would want to relax with some buddies. Often though, they had plans, and those plans spelled Couple with a capital "C." The self-doubt had to do with all my past relationships and wondering about my part in that. The assumption that annoyed me the most? That I was somehow not OK in my uncoupled state, that I should be seeking *the* cure (a partner).

How did I explain my single state to myself? Initially, coming out of a five-year relationship, I was determined to do some soul searching. I was fed up with myself for being better at terminating relationships than maintaining them. For years I had explained breakups and partner changing with: "She's just not the right one for me." It was time to examine my own role in relationships. Little did I know I would extend this examination period to twelve years. I think I'm a slow learner. As the years went by, I noticed that I still wasn't doing anything about finding another lover. It felt right for me to be single. Sure, sometimes I longed for that familiar and intimate other, but starting a new relationship drew a blank. In my case, I saw my singleness as self-chosen.

So back to that Friday night—I have no plans, I want to play, and I want company—and not the company of strangers. However, my coupled friends are otherwise engaged. Loneliness arises with a tinge of self-pity. Now, I find the victim role as tempting as the next woman, and I've spent my share of time there. But years in the women's movement and a few in therapy have come between me and sweet victimhood. I would just have to figure this one out. If I wanted to have company on weekends, I had to plan in advance. And if I didn't feel like making plans, I could damn well draw on my own resources, maybe spend some time relaxing—time alone recovering from my job or thinking about my life.

Of course I still envied my friends in couples when it seemed like the weekend stretched out barren before me. This brings me to one of my favorite ploys when in a relationship: I wanted her to take care of my needs, and I tended to blame her for whatever was going wrong between us. Part of the beauty for me in being single was that there was no one around to blame. I was all I had. Blaming couples for my loneliness wasn't very satisfying. I tried hanging out with a couple conveniently located in my neighborhood, but I soon saw they often needed their weekend time to process their own crises. And, I agree, it feels lousy to be shut out by a couple when you're alone. But they weren't the social workers assigned to my case, and I didn't particularly want anyone spending time with me out of pity.

I did manage to use my demanding job and difficult single status to shirk some responsibilities toward friends. One of them had the nerve to confront me. That sent me back to the self-examination room (after a good round of self-loathing). Resources such as therapy and books are so handy in a crisis: at that point I read *Dance of Intimacy*, by Harriet Lerner (1989). I wasn't in a lover-type intimate relationship, but I didn't want to lose this friend. So I began to follow Lerner's advice in tending relationships with family origin first, looking there for the snags in my relationship patterns, and for the slow path to a healthy relationship with myself.

This is not to say there weren't assumptions that I rejected. One distant family member (let's call him Hank), while accepting my lesbianism, seemed very uncomfortable with my singleness. Whenever we talked on the phone (every few months), he would ask if I had found a honey, or was seeing someone, or some such. It irritated me. I finally asked why this was so important to him. Well, he said, he wanted me to be happy (and being in a couple ensures that?). I asked if he had a problem with me being single and happy, and told him I just might be single the rest of my life. He finally owned that *he* needed a relationship to function comfortably and assumed I did too.

Lesbian acquaintances occasionally did things I didn't appreciate: the gift of JoAnn Loulan's book, *Lesbian Passion*, at a birthday, the attempts to match me up with anyone handy, and the comment, "She's so nice. Why isn't she with someone?" What happened to the idea that a woman is a whole being, not half a couple?

How do we handle such attitudes? Perhaps by gently questioning the person's assumptions and generalizations, or by just having a talk: "How do you feel about me being single?" But there is no doubt that some women in couples are wary of single lesbians. Maybe we remind them of their own fears of loneliness. And, as single lesbians, we can be resentful of coupled women. Whichever side we stand on, we shy away from the "other" and feel at ease with those who share common ground.

In fact, we need to extend that common ground, and bridge boundaries of marital status, as well as those of sexual preference, race, and so on. For me, I wanted to stay "unattached" in order to become more connected to myself and to explore the grounds of relationships with friends, with family, with colleagues. I needed time to sort the hill of seeds and pebbles that were my life thus far, to descend to my underground regions and negotiate new arrangements with my demons and guardians. Many of those weekends alone, while painful, bore fruit in my snail-like search for internal balance.

Whether single by design or by fate, what *matters* is how we work with that state. Like other states that may visit us (chronic illness, loss of loved ones, disasters at work, deafness, and so on) we can call them curse or opportunity. I see three avenues for us singles. We can bemoan our single state; we can rail at couples for not inviting us to their parties; and/or, we can figure out how to live a full life. Inevitably, I did some of the first two, but didn't see the point of spending my life there.

Speaking of the rest of my life, would I always be single? I began to ask myself that question when the years of celibacy stretched on, with no end in sight. "Will I ever have a lover relationship again?" There was no answer, but in that present moment I felt no urge to couple. I had to trust myself and let the future take care of itself. I came to accept the possibility of lifetime celibacy with equanimity.

Yet now a lover has entered my story once more. Does that mean I was lost before and now am found? Hardly. Were all those years a preparation for this, the true goal? Not really. It's true that I am happy. But that came first. Being in a couple is not the source of my happiness; I had already found my sources of happiness as a single woman. And therefore, I feel better equipped to enjoy a relationship.

Developing or finding that happiness, however, took time and hard work. Year after year, inch by inch, I remodeled my connections with family members, moving from old lies and phoniness toward honesty and authenticity. I shifted my relationship to work from one of stress and overload to a lighter, more playful one. I benefited tremendously (and continue to do so) from friendships with women who, like me, were struggling to shed old pain and live a clearer, calmer, more conscious life. Some of these women were in couples, some not. Sharing our stories extended the common ground between us.

Friendship is indispensable to a single lesbian. And friends *can* be found, even coupled ones. After all, there is a considerable range among couples: those who have *no* social life—not easy to make friends with; those who socialize but always as a unit—if you like them, have them over for dinner; and those who enjoy independent friendships—a good source of friendships.

Clearly, most of one's needs can be met outside the couple structure. In fact, it seems that we lesbians get into trouble in our couples when we try to get all our needs met by the partner. For social contact, one can diversify: hang out with the lesbians who are open to it, and branch out beyond the lesbian community. To feel needed, we can give time to those populations that need help: kids, elderly, those who are challenged, sick, dying, homeless. For touch, in additions to hugs, I love body work.

In the final analysis, being single can be a very rich experience, for a lesbian as for anyone . . . if we let the experience take us back to our core, to what we want to feel, express, provide to others in our daily lives. In Linda's *Love Matters* columns, even the problems of relationship often lead one back to the self, to our core. I found a spaciousness and flexibility in the single life that I needed for my exploration and healing. This freedom could be used in many ways: living abroad for a while, taking part in a project (political, humanitarian, ecological, etc.), going back to school, writing poetry . . . the possibilities are endless.

So, flex your wings, singles. Do you need a new direction, stillness, truth, balance, kinship, adventure? Whatever your passions, your interests, your loves, give yourself the gift of exploring them. And couples, check in with your single friends to find out how life looks from their perspective.

In the meantime, don't ever forget, loving friendships among lesbians matter too.

A loving friend

I did live, as I said, with one person for a long time. And I loved that communion and that routine and that coming together in the evening and having a drink and talking. This is very precious. I miss it. I am terribly lonely now, but I have also become enamoured of solitude. That's my last great love.

May Sarton
from *World of Light:*
A Portrait of May Sarton
by Martha Simpson and Martha Wheelock

Busyness

Question: I read your column some months and wonder where you and Maureen get the time to have a relationship? My partner, Gloria, and I are middle-aged with what seems like such busy, overwhelming lives. Both of us have full-time-plus jobs, a home in constant need of attention, some friends and social life, and aging parents. We seem to fall into bed exhausted having hardly had the time to say good night. As much as we want to spend time together, time seems to be the enemy of our relationship. How do you and Maureen do it—find time for your relationship given the demands of the rest of your lives?

Joyce

Answer:

We awaken in the morning, startled by the alarm clock, groggy from not enough sleep, anxious about what needs to be done today, guilty about what didn't get done yesterday. We jump out of bed, try to squeeze in some exercise, make a few calls, throw something together that resembles breakfast and fly out the door hoping to arrive at work in time for our first appointments. Life has become a race against time, and we all feel as if we're losing. "Time for a relationship," you say; "You must be kidding!"

Oh my! Whatever has become of our lives? I am astounded at how often I hear couples complain that they never see each other, or never have a minute alone with each other, or feel so stressed out that they can't enjoy their time together. Joyce's lament is an all-too-common relationship issue. No matter how fast we go, how effective and efficient we are, there is never enough time for all we have signed on to do. And, when push comes to shove, it's our time with each other that too often is sacrificed. In our so-called Western civilization, it seems as if there's a social, economic, and technological conspiracy to keep us busy. Conspiracy or not, *busyness* is seriously undermining the intimacy in our closest relationships. Although it can be argued that many factors influence our choices about how we spend our time (such as desire, fear, compatibility, commitment), it is also true that many couples such as Joyce and Gloria sincerely want to spend more time together—if they could just figure out how.

So, how do Maureen and I do it—because it's true that we do preserve and protect our time together—despite the demands of the rest of our lives? I'm proud and pleased to say that I think we do a better job of it than most. For us, time together is simply a top priority 'and the first order of business in our hectic lives. Both of us are acutely aware of how easily a relationship can get neglected in the stressful, multifaceted, fast-paced lives we lead. Our relationship is the sanctuary that we need to find peace in the middle of this madness. Maureen and I don't *find* time for our relationship so much as we *make* time. Time together feels less like a luxury than it does a *necessity*. Maureen and I are committed, not only to *having* a relationship, but to *being* in one. All of these requirements take a lot of time. A lot of time is what we give to them.

How, then, do we make the time for each other? Whenever, however, and wherever we can. We make it every morning over coffee. We make it for lunch on the run at Poor Richard's. We make it sipping martinis on the Broadmoor patio. We make it bumping butts in the claw-footed tub. We make it chasing rainbows and hot air balloons. We make it on a walk around the block when dusk is falling. We make it on the beach at Cannon Beach every October. We make it late in the evening underneath the covers. Our time together may be scheduled or spontaneous, ritualistic or haphazard, brief or luxurious, peaceful or tumultuous, mundane or richly satisfying. It hardly seems to matter. We continue to choose time with each other— again and again.

That I would come to value a partnership enough, to be willing to devote so much time and attention, is nothing short of a miracle and a blessing. Maureen came into this relationship knowing the value of leisure, of hanging out, of time spent with loved ones. I, on the other hand, came into our relationship obsessed by work, compelled by activity, and leery of love. Busyness was a deeply embedded way of life, a *noble* calling. Without being aware of it at the time, busyness had been a refuge against fear, sadness, anger, emptiness, inadequacy, confusion and, most powerfully, my best defense against intimacy. My love for Maureen became a healing arena for my wounded heart.

As you can imagine, my busy way of life gets dramatically challenged in my relationship with Maureen. It's not that she actively *tries* to change me . . . it's just that her more laid-back approach appears to be contagious. Maybe I'm too old to lose any more time. Maybe I've finally figured out what really matters. Maybe I'm just with the world's greatest playmate. Whatever the reason(s), hanging out with Maureen is a heck of a lot more fun than being busy.

Our relationship has taught me that, for even the most hard-core busyness addict, there exists a tiny spark of longing—for play, for joy, for leisure. If I can learn to fan that flame, I'm certain that Joyce and Gloria—with mindfulness and their pure need—can find their own path to a calmer life.

> The best use of our time is being generous and really present with others. . . . But if we do not have time for the people we love, if we cannot make ourselves available to them, how can we say that we love them?
>
> Thich Nhat Hanh
> *Living Buddha, Living Christ*

In the meantime, don't ever forget, your love matters.

At work you think of the children you have left at home. At home, you think of the work you've left unfinished. Such a struggle is unleashed within yourself. Your heart is rent.

Golda Meir
quoted by Orianna Fallaci in *L'Europa*
cited in *The Beacon Book of Quotations by Women*
by Rosalie Maggio

Saying Good-Bye

Question: My live-in partner of eight years, "Sue," has just dumped me for another woman. Despite knowing that our relationship was waning (and doing nothing about it), I feel completely devastated. Angry, betrayed, jealous, confused, guilty, inadequate, and terribly, terribly sad. I vacillate between wanting to wring Sue's neck and wanting to beg her to stay. We had been friends even before we became lovers, so the loss feels monumental. Sue still wants to be friends and, when I'm not in the anger mode, I do too. She's even suggested therapy to help us terminate. I want to be able to keep communicating but some of what she says is so painful that it feels as if my heart is breaking. Yet, I care enough about Sue, myself, and what we had together to try to get some resolution. I'd like to end this relationship with some semblance of grace, even though I am not really ready for it to end. Can you suggest anything that might help me manage this breakup—any tools, any skills? Do you think friendship is possible (or even practical) under these circumstances? Do you see any value in therapy after the fact?

Elizabeth

Answer: Elizabeth, you're certainly off to a good start. For you to even want to end your relationship with grace is, in itself, an act of grace. Congratulations, you're on the right track. I had several significant relationships before I met Maureen (including a legal marriage). Looking back now, I can see that, while I struggled toward grace, the ending of each of those relationships was not only graceless, it was often merciless, clumsy, undignified—even mean. Because the relationships themselves lacked sufficient love, or awareness, or willingness, their endings naturally reflected that. You seem to be ahead of the game by wanting to terminate this relationship in a conscious manner with all the elements of a graceful ending in place.

All that leaves for me to do is reinforce the direction your inner wisdom is taking you and share some of what I've learned from my own breakup experiences after (and I'm talking *years* after) the fact. I truly admire the efforts that you and Sue are making, and I fully appreciate how difficult those efforts are.

> It is only through letting our heart break that we discover something unexpected: The heart cannot actually *break*, it can only break *open*.
>
> John Welwood
> *Love and Awakening*

In the first place, you seem willing to keep your heart open despite having so many conflicted and difficult feelings—sadness, anger, guilt, and betrayal. Separation and loss are so incredibly painful, we need to take an adequate amount of time to mourn (regardless of what shape the relationship was in). We enter a relationship with hearts full of promise and with hopes and dreams of happiness and permanence. We leave a relationship with tremendous disappointment, discouragement, disillusionment, and feelings of failure. I'm glad that you're able to identify your feelings, and yet I hope that you don't become too identified *with* them. They are only fluid, impermanent states of mind and, as much as we need to feel them, we don't need to get too attached to them. I cringe (and that's on a *good* day) when I recall my own attachment to my feelings during some of my breakups. Whether playing out my feelings as the Drama Queen (being manipulative, threatening, or hysterical) or the Ice Queen (repressing, burying, being stoic or heartless), I was overidentified with my feelings—terrified of them or resisting them. To paraphrase Mr. Rogers, wishing things won't make them come true. So, we can all breathe a sigh of relief that you're only *thinking* about wringing Sue's neck. Believe me, I've had more treacherous thoughts (and less noble behavior) when I've been in the process of breaking up. You know, I like to think of myself as a moderately dignified person, but when you feel as if your heart is broken, well . . . dignity schmignity. Don't tell anyone I told you this, but I've staked out buildings, contemplated suicide by Häagen-Dazs overdose, played the same song over and over until friends ran screaming from my house, called my agent to find out *exactly* how much life insurance money I'd get if I were lucky enough to become a widow, spent money I couldn't afford on things I didn't even like, cried enough to induce a sinus infection and *wallowed*—like a pig in mud—in the grief, injustice, and pure misery of a relationship's demise.

The most excruciating breakups involved being dumped for Someone Else. That pain was absolutely unbearable. Recently, a friend told me that she learned everything she needed to know about breaking up after she got dumped in eighth grade. "Always be the first to leave," she says. Losing someone to death is, indeed, a heart-breaking experience. Being abandoned, though, just sort of slices your heart to ribbons. Your heart, Elizabeth, has been lacerated. You may need time out to integrate the shock and to stabilize your emotions. But, by being willing to let your *heart break open*, you're on your way to real healing.

> There is nothing wrong with asking where I've gone wrong in a "failed" relationship. Trouble appears only when that examination is not honest or does not go deep enough.
>
> Thomas Moore
> *Soul Mates*

You seem willing to frame this breakup in a mindful way, with honesty, awareness, and compassion. You admit that the relationship was waning, that neither of you was doing anything about it, that you still care about Sue, that you're looking for resolution. I think, Elizabeth, that you have all the skills you need—far more than I had when I needed them the most. As much as I *wanted* to be mindful, my fear and anger would get the best of me. I felt defensive and on the attack too much of the time. Back then, I didn't have tools. I had weapons—criticism, judgment, condemnation (of myself and others). My need for blame was so deeply imbedded that it took a therapeutic crowbar to excavate it. I saw people as good/bad, right/wrong, victim/perpetrator, and that's how I thought about each of my breakups. It took (and is taking) many years of working on myself, my psychic pain, my self-esteem, and my self-image before I could arrive at a more enlightened view of relationships. Today, I believe that all relationships are *co-created*—from their beginnings to their endings. I no longer see people as either dump*ers* or dump*ees*. I played an active part in the endings of all my prior relationships regardless of who was calling it quits. Mindful thinking is the most effective tool to use when your relationship is ending, as you seem to intuitively know. I see that clearly in your desire for understanding and resolution. I see it in your open heart and thoughtfulness. By your willingness to dig around in the breakup muck, you're demonstrating your readiness to let this experience be transformative in your life.

Finally, Elizabeth, I sense your need to honor and sanctify this relationship—to *somehow* arrive at grace. That's why you're still talking to Sue, why you're considering therapy, why you're writing to me. As I look back at my own breakups, I think that my divorce most closely met the need for the kind of closure you'd like to have. It's ironic, given how painful it was, how cynical I felt about divorce laws at that time, and how ambivalent I still feel about legalizing relationships. Nevertheless, my divorce provided a formal, legal, definitive way to *signify* the end of my marriage while providing rituals that acknowledged its importance. The divorce was preceded by a separation of over a year—time in which to reflect on the marriage and its fate. Once our decision was made, we had to negotiate about custody and disposition of property, and write up a divorce contract. We actually had to show up in court and say out loud, in front of a judge, that our relationship was irretrievable. In spite of the resistance I had to all of these rituals, they provided the formality, the finality, the sanction that the ending of any significant relationship truly deserves. My ex-husband and I even went out to breakfast after our court appearance. Choosing a restaurant where we'd shared many happy times, we laughed, cried, said good-bye, and celebrated the end of our marriage. I've come to believe that ritual, ceremony, and celebration are as important to the end of a relationship as they are to the beginning. Too many lesbian relationships lack that ritual on either end.

We live in a culture in which we are invisible. There are no institutionalized rituals for women who love women. Without engagements and weddings, we're left to *invent* our anniversaries. Is it the day of our first kiss, the night we first slept together, the day we moved in together, opened a joint checking account, gave each other rings, what? While I've seen an increase in commitment ceremonies, marriages, and anniversary celebrations among lesbians, it is more often true that our relationships lack witnessing, honoring, ritualizing. And, if it's a challenge to mark our beginnings, what about the endings? The endings are equally vague. Was it the day I told her I felt as if I didn't love her anymore, the day she found me in bed with someone else, the night I returned the house keys? While divorce doesn't guarantee resolution, it certainly has definition. It's a tangible event involving the solemnity of the courtroom, the payment of lawyers, intimidating documents, and, whether you're ready or not, *finality*—an end to the way things were.

Ritual can be a powerful tool when terminating a relationship. Elizabeth, if you and Sue go to therapy, it may feel like a ritual. Perhaps it will be a way for you to honor the relationship that you had. Perhaps it will help you achieve grace. You can share your stories, bring in your photos, yell and scream and stomp your feet. You can cry and grieve and have your relationship—its power and its pain—witnessed. Regrettably, I have witnessed the end of many lesbian relationships in my office. Sometimes there is nothing for me to do but hug the women and cry with them. I feel as if I should be lighting candles, creating altars, solemnly presiding over a divorce ceremony. I think, maybe next time, I'll suggest that. So, Elizabeth, one of the paths to grace is ritual. You can create and experience ritual with or without Sue. I hope, though, that you'll both want to be present because it can offer incredible healing.

In regard to friendship—its possibilities and practicalities—there's no universal advice that will be a perfect fit for you and Sue. When I *desired* friendships with former lovers, I sought it—sometimes successfully, sometimes not. Sometimes, though, I didn't *want* to be friends, or I didn't feel willing to produce the energy or do the work that such a friendship would require. It's a very personal decision—no protocols, no rules, no one right way to proceed. You have only your heart to guide you.

In your case, Elizabeth, I'm confident that you're in good hands—your own. I think you'll find all the answers you need to whatever questions are raised by this process you're going through.

For me, your questions began my own small journey as I revisited my prior relationships and the passages they represented. Believe it or not, I'm incredibly grateful to each of my former partners. I encountered some pain that still needs attending and some good times that still deserve celebration. Thank you, Elizabeth, for the gift of those memories.

In the meantime, don't ever forget, your love matters.

If you lose your lover

If you lose your lover
rain hurt you. blackbirds
brood over the sky trees
burn down everywhere brown
rabbits run under
car wheels. should your
body cry? to feel such
blue and empty bed dont
bother. if you lose your
lover comb hair go here
or there get   another

Judy Grahn
The Work of a Common Woman

My Turn

Maureen Stevens

I can't say whether it was conscious or unconscious, spoken of directly or indirectly understood. However, at some point during the last three years, Linda and I came to feel that this body of work wouldn't be complete if you didn't hear something from me.

Who else would tell you what it's been like to watch Linda conceive, gestate, give birth to, agonize over, nurture, stay up all night with, coddle, cajole, cry about, scream at, withdraw from, laugh at, suffer through, and burst with pride over this writing project.

I thought about doing a "How Do I Love Thee, Let Me Count The Ways" kind of column. It would be the format in which I would tell you how precious and adorable Linda is, how magically her brilliance and intuition blend, how she is actually the one who hung the sun, the moon, and the stars. I'm afraid, though, that I would get sappy, and mushy, and a little sickening about my profound love, respect, and gratitude for her. I'm afraid, too, that some of you may not believe in miracles or matches made in heaven. So I am resisting the temptation to go there.

At first, the whole notion that the most intimate details of our private lives might be revealed and force us—and *me*, for God's sake—to publicly go deeper into our coming-out process, was about as attractive as a nuclear attack. Linda is persuasive, though; and eventually I came to share her vision— that the column offered us a wonderful opportunity to explore the questions and issues in our own relationship. Ultimately, I was able to give my blessing because I trusted that Linda would convey the honesty, the difficulty, the goofiness and, most important, the sacredness of our lives together. I believe that she has achieved that—and more.

The blood, sweat, and tears that spilled over this book have been referred to in some of the columns. What is really difficult to explain, however, is how much it has changed our lives.

We have *lived* each question from every possible angle. From each rough draft to each neatly typed column, we engaged in a process that probably would not otherwise have happened. We discussed, argued, watched old belief systems crumble (and created new ones), laughed and cried over every issue that every question from a reader brought up. The process *itself* challenged us to develop a deeper level of communication, understanding, intimacy, and playfulness—all under the guise of meeting a deadline.

In the name of research, I put defenses and opinions aside and engaged in heated discussions that, for a less noble cause (such as day-to-day living), I would normally shy away from. Now, of course, I'm wondering if this whole project was Linda's way of tricking me into doing work that I would (probably) never have done!

Having said that, I will tell you that I *am* glad that this book project is behind us and I get to see my girlfriend again on the weekends! I am delighted, though, that all of you are getting a glimpse of the tender heart, the open mind, the quick wit, the emotional courage, the intellect, the integrity, and the authenticity of the woman with whom I share my heart and home.

P. S. Of course, don't ever forget that your love matters.

Woman

I dream of a place between your breasts
to build my house like a haven
where I plant crops
in your body
an endless harvest
where the commonest rock
is moonstone and ebony opal
giving milk to all of my hungers
and your night comes down upon me
like a nurturing rain.

Audre Lorde
The Black Unicorn

My So-Called Ending

Be patient toward all that is unsolved in your heart and try to live the *questions themselves* like locked rooms or books that are written in a foreign tongue. The point is to live everything. *Live* the questions now. Perhaps you will then gradually, without noticing it, live your way some distant day into the answers.

Rainer Maria Rilke
quoted in *Journey of the Heart*
by John Welwood

I'm sitting here, close to tears, wondering how on earth I'm ever going to write this ending and what will become of me—and this book—if I can't. The Goddess knows how hard I've tried (and so does poor Maureen) for over six weeks now, page after page, version after bloody version, all falling short of the mark, somehow. Too flat—too meager—too book-reportish—too blah, blah, blah. I know what I want this ending to do. I want it to capture the heart of the story. I know how I want this ending to feel. I want it to feel like a grand finale. Yet it seems too difficult to convey this experience—its enormity, its impact, its meaning—while I'm still in the midst of *having it*. I feel like a newspaper reporter trying to meet the city desk deadline while the story itself is still unfolding. But my contract with The Haworth Press states that my manuscript is due, in their office, on March 31, 1998. So, ready or not, it's time to put the icing on the cake. I had no idea it would feel like this at the end. But why should I be surprised? Writing *Love Matters* hasn't been anything at all like I imagined.

I thought I was writing a column, but the column turned into a book. Big difference. It was as if I thought I was going to have a brief affair with Maureen sixteen years ago, and the brief affair turned into marriage. Columns/affairs—they don't require much besides starry eyes, adrenalin, and innocence. Books/marriages—they require much more, such as road maps, commitments, and courage. If I had known what either actually entailed, I'm not sure I could have consciously signed on. No one—no experts, gurus, or guides—could ever adequately prepare one for these journeys. They take you into the deep, dark recesses of the mind and require all that you can possibly be.

I *thought*, when I began this column, that I already knew how to write. I had written all of my life. I considered it to be pretty easy. I had even taught others to write. It turned out that I was hopelessly naive. There were a number of factors I left out of the equation. Yes, years ago I was a fluid and fluent writer. I could sit at this very same typewriter pounding away—armed with endless *facts* and *opinions* about the external world; and I had the self-righteousness, certainty, and conviction that facts and opinions engender. Today, I sit facing a white, empty page, and I am disarmed by the internal world of *feelings* and *beliefs* and the uncertainty, confusion, and humility that feelings and beliefs engender. That is, on days when I can even figure out how I feel or what I believe! When I began this column three years ago, I thought I knew how I felt—about myself, my life, and my relationships. I yak about my feelings all day long. Yet once I had to commit my feelings to the written page—for any and all to read—I could no longer trust my feelings or trust my feelings with the world. All of this made the writing process risky, painstaking and, some days, absolutely impossible.

I *thought* I had more than enough ideas to write columns for the rest of my life. It never occurred to me that I would have too many. I would lasso an idea and wrestle it to the ground but, before I knew it, the idea had me pinned to the ground. I would begin the day excited about an idea and, like a kid chasing butterflies, I would follow this one, then that one, then the next, fooled into thinking the best was yet to come. Harnessing my thoughts was like catching lightening bolts in a jar. It was maddening.

I *thought* I'd be answering other people's questions about *their* lives. I never expected to be living the questions *myself*. Whatever issue I was responding to, however far removed it first appeared, became a mirror, a question about my life, a personal quest. "Who am I?" I kept asking in relationship to each question and "What is it that I believe?"

I *thought* I had a good enough relationship with Maureen. Writing this book challenged us to have an even better one. Each column served as an instrument to keep us talking and working the relationship issues. *Love Matters* became an in-house therapist forcing us to live the questions now.

I *thought* I was up to the task of writing—that there was a strong enough *me*. But my demons—an obsessive nature, an insatiable search for the truth, and relentless self-doubt—kept conspiring to thwart the creative spirit in me. I was forced to dig deeper all of the time, look for a more essential nature, speak from a more authentic voice. I had to become a warrior.

I *thought* I'd be in cyberspace by now—processing rather than typing words, surfing the net instead of the dictionary, e-mailing rather than telephoning my friends. It was not to be. I actually bought a Gateway 2000, but I never learned how to use it. Writing a book was such uncharted territory, I needed the safety of a comfortable old shoe. My IBM Selectric provided that comfort to the very end.

I *thought* I knew a thing or two about the human heart and what it is about love that really *matters*. My heart has broken open time and again, writing this column, as I witnessed other people's stories and lived through my own. I've come to understand, through these experiences, that the heart is indeed a sanctuary, that love is nothing less than a sacrament, and that writing about love is a devotional practice. And, in the rarest of moments when my heart feels completely open and my center is very still, it actually feels as if *love* is *my very essence.*

I *thought,* of course, that I'd be ready to let go of this book when I got to the end. I had no idea how reluctant I would actually be. I feel like a mother sending her precious, little daughter off to her first day of school—proud, but scared—smoothing her hair, tying her bows, polishing her shoes, praying that everyone will love her as much as I do.

Who knew this column would take me on a *Magical Mystery Tour?* No one could write the lyrics for that (except the Beatles, of course).

Well, here I am at my so-called ending, knowing full well that there is no end: no end to relationship questions, yours or mine; and no end, at least in sight, to my thinking and writing about them. I may be tired, but I'm not quite finished.

So, keep your cards and letters coming in care of Linda Sutton, *New Phazes,* P. O. Box 6485, Colorado Springs, Colorado 80934-6485.

In the meantime, don't ever forget, your love matters.

— *Love Matters* —

Love Matters, Inc., came into being to celebrate and support lesbian and gay relationships. All the artwork found throughout this book and on its cover is part of a greeting card collection. For a catalog on this line of greeting cards and related stationery products (as well as information concerning online *Love Matters* advice and *Love Matters* workshops), write to Love Matters, Inc., c/o P. O. Box 7984, Colorado Springs, CO 80933-7984, or e-mail lovematters@compuserve.com.

Bibliography

Allen, Mary and David M. Edwards. (1997). "Depression Out of the Closet," *Treatment Today,* Spring 1997, Vol. 9, No. 2, pp. 6-7.

Allison, Dorothy. (1983). *The Women Who Hate Me: Poetry 1980-1990.* Ithaca, New York: Firebrand Books.

Berzon, Betty. (1988). *Permanent Partners: Building Gay & Lesbian Relationships That Last.* New York: Plume, Penguin Group.

Bettelheim, Bruno. (1987). *A Good Enough Parent: A Book on Child-Rearing.* New York: Alfred A. Knopf, p. ix.

Blumstein, Philip and Pepper Schwartz. (1983). *American Couples: Money, Work, Sex.* New York: William Morrow and Company, Inc., p. 322.

Borges, Phil, photographs, text by His Holiness the Dalai Lama, prologue by Jeffery Hopkins, epilogue by Elie Wiesel. (1996). *Tibetan Portrait: The Power of Compassion.* New York: Rizzoli International Publications, Inc.

Brown, Rita Mae. (1998). *Starting from Scratch: A Different Kind of Writer's Manual.* New York: Bantam Books.

Chambers, Jane. (1984). *Warrior at Rest.* New York: TNT Classics.

Clunis, D. Merilee and G. Dorsey Green. (1988). *Lesbian Couples.* Seattle: Seal Press.

Cole, Ellen. (1993). "Lesbians at Menopause." *A Friend Indeed,* Vol. IX, No. 9, February 1993, pp. 1-3.

Cole, Ellen and Rothblum, Esther. (1991). "Lesbian Sex at Menopause: as Good or Better Than Ever." In Sang, Barbara, Joyce Warshow, and Adrienne J. Smith, eds. *Lesbians at Midlife: The Creative Transition—An Anthology.* San Francisco: Spinsters Book Company, pp. 184-193.

Coss, Clare, ed. (1996). *The Arc of Love: An Anthology of Lesbian Love Poems.* New York: Scribner.

Grahn, Judy. (1978). *The Work of a Common Woman.* New York: St. Martin's Press.

Greer, Germaine. (1991). *The Change: Women, Aging, and the Menopause.* New York: Faucet-Columbine, Ballantine Books.

Hearon, Shelby. (1996). *Footprints.* New York: Random House.

Johnson, Susan E. (1991). *Staying Power: Long-Term Lesbian Couples.* Tallahassee, FL: The Naiad Press.

Koller, Alice. (1981). *An Unknown Woman: A Journey to Self-Discovery.* New York: Bantam Books.

Kübler-Ross, Elisabeth. (1969). *On Death and Dying.* New York: Touchstone Books, Simon and Schuster.

Lamott, Anne. (1997). *Crooked Little Heart.* New York: Pantheon.

Lapidus, Jacqueline. (1977). *Starting Over.* Milford, CT: Out and Out Books.

Lerner, Harriet. (1989). *Dance of Intimacy: A Woman's Guide to Courageous Acts of Change in Key Relationships.* New York: Harper & Row Publishers.

Levine, Stephen. (1982). *Who Dies? An Investigation of Conscious Living and Conscious Dying.* Garden City, NY: Anchor Press/Doubleday.

Levine, Stephen. (1987). *Healing into Life and Death.* New York: Anchor Press/Doubleday.

Levine, Stephen and Ondrea Levine. (1995). *Embracing the Beloved: A Relationship As a Path of Awakening.* New York: Doubleday.

Lorde, Audre. (1978). *The Black Unicorn.* New York: W. W. Norton & Co., Inc.

Loulan, JoAnn. (1987). *Lesbian Passion: Loving Ourselves and Each Other.* San Francisco: Spinsters/Aunt Lute Book Company, p. 33.

Maggio, Rosalie. (1992). *The Beacon Book of Quotations by Women.* Boston: Beacon Press, pp. 13, 74.

Moore, Thomas. (1992). *Care of the Soul: A Guide for Cultivating Depth and Sacredness in Everyday Life.* New York: HarperCollins Publishers.

Moore, Thomas. (1994). "The Care of a Marriage." *New Age Journal,* January-February 1994, pp. 58-59.

Moore, Thomas. (1994). *Soul Mates: Honoring the Mysteries of Love and Relationship.* New York: HarperCollins Publishers.

Morgan, Robin. (1990). *Upstairs in the Garden: Poems Selected and New, 1968-1988.* New York: W. W. Norton & Company.

Murray, Michael T. (1996). *Natural Alternatives to Prozac.* New York: William Morrow and Company, Inc.

Nhat Hanh, Thich. (1995). *Living Buddha, Living Christ.* New York: Riverhead Books, G. P. Putnam's Sons.

Ocamb, Karen. (1997). "When a Kiss Is More Than Just a Kiss." *The Lesbian News,* Vol. 22, No. 9, April 1997, pp. 22-24.

Pace, Anita L., ed. (1992). *Write from the Heart: Lesbians Healing from Heartache—An Anthology.* Beaverton, OR: Baby Steps Press.

Papolos, Demitri and Janice Papolos. (1997). *Overcoming Depression: The Definitive Resource for Patients and Families Who Live with Depression and Manic-Depression,* Third Edition. New York: Harper Perennial, a division of HarperCollins Publishers.

Pogrebin, Letty Cottin. (1997). "Endless Love." *Ms.,* Vol. VIII, No. 2, September-October 1997, p. 36.

Pratt, Minnie Bruce. (1985). *We Say We Love Each Other.* Ithaca, New York: Firebrand Books.

Replansky, Naomi. (1994). *The Dangerous World.* Chicago, IL: Another Chicago Press.

Rosen, Laura Epstein and Xavier Francisco Amador. (1997). *When Someone You Love Is Depressed: How to Help Your Loved One Without Losing Yourself.* New York: A Fireside Trade Paperback, Simon and Schuster, Inc.

Simpson, Martha and Martha Wheelock. (1982). *World of Light: A Portrait of May Sarton—with additional poems and comments.* New York: Ishtar Enterprises.

Styron, William. (1990). *Darkness Visible: A Memoir of Madness.* New York: Random House, Inc., p. 57.

Welwood, John, ed. (1985). *Challenge of the Heart: Love, Sex, and Intimacy in Changing Times.* Boston: Shambhala Press, pp. 258, 261.

Welwood, John. (1990). *Journey of the Heart: Intimate Relationship and the Path of Love.* New York: HarperCollins Publishers, pp. 1, 124-125.

Welwood, John. (1996). *Love and Awakening: Discovering the Sacred Path of Intimate Relationship.* New York: HarperCollins Publishers.